Warranted

By

Anca Dumitrescu

Warranted

Anca Dumitrescu
Copyright 2016

ISBN: 978-0-615-25400-5

P_{art} O_{ne}

On November 3rd, 2014, my mother died of heart failure, in Bucharest, Romania. She had been diagnosed with inoperable lung cancer earlier that fall. Several days later my friend Mr.Greulich, who had become my father figure after my own father's death in 2007, died of cancer in Cranford. I did not go to say goodbye to my mother.

March 2015. Letter to my mother. Thank you, mother, for the unlikeliest of circumstances: since your death I am finally able to accept myself as bipolar. In group, this morning, I talked about what it takes to turn things around, even at a late date, about that point of acceptance beyond which old damaging behavior doesn't have to be repeated anymore. Every time I'm in a group now talking about it, I know that it couldn't have happened until your passing. It's that lesson life presented to me, over and over again, until I got it. Now that I can't argue with you anymore, it's time to let that lesson sink in.

What a rude awakening, to find out that in so many ways I was still arguing with you these past thirteen years, when I thought I'd stopped back then, at the advice of the last doctor I'd seen in the hospital. Did it have to rewind all the way down to a hospitalization before it could come up so clearly? What was I trying to prove, not taking my lithium? That maybe I was being mistaken for a sick person instead of being one, after all? The same old game we played for so long, mother. Now with your death I am at a point of reckoning unlike any other: dealing with how much I've distanced myself from my own life.

Months ago I distanced myself from work contacts and social contacts, limited as they were. I now find myself at a loss as to how to proceed. I need to rebuild a support structure on a more stable foundation than in the past. I am floundering. And yet it is my life, for the first time without disastrous consequences – I still have a home, my cats, my things, money to live on for the time being.

With a near-catastrophe averted, the thing to look for is the sum of old patterns of anger and frustration, so as not to enter them again. I will ask for help in finding a job; I will ask for help with the shift in health insurance since I'm losing my right to the one I have now. I will do so without acting desperate. The situation is not hopeless. *Helpless but not hopeless*, like the old Recovery *spotting* goes. Pen and paper will help, using that positive pattern of regeneration. I have skills to use that I have put aside for years. It's time to draw on them again.

A little later on I will go to the dollar store, the one I like so much, to buy myself a notebook so I can begin to write again more than on scraps that I quickly discard. Part of the shut-down has been this need to "erase the evidence", which I need to back away from slowly. Erasing the evidence by not writing at all for long stretches has been going on for three years, since I stopped seeing my doctor. I had something to hide after that, and the pattern finally led to this last hospitalization six weeks ago, after thirteen years of staying clear. I derailed, almost as if I were following a plan.

I probably made the cats nervous, moving furniture around, feeling unsettled. Today, here we are, all four of us, they taking it easy with me here in the living room. I am sitting in the armchair with paper in my lap and pen in hand. It has been hard, with the medication settling in, facing the dread of picking up the pieces again.

At first, the groups felt like punishment. Now things are better. Today I was able to see that all of us are different, and at different stages of coping with our own respective illnesses. Seeing this last bit is important, realizing that it was all necessary so that the struggle would have to finally be over between us, mother, before I could understand how much help I really need. I do, now, and it just is what it is.

Like with my inability to clear things up between dad and me as he was nearing his death, I was unable to have a good relationship with you, mother, as you neared your death. I have failed more than friends. I have failed my family. With Alex it doesn't feel the same, though there is the sense of failure there too, mostly because of the lack of communication these past eight years. But when it comes to you, I've failed clearly, mom.

Is this what continues to bring such a deep sense of loss? That I failed to have a relationship with both my parents? The relationships were there, they were just very difficult, and as the case was with you, mom, very damaging. So, as to move forward now, I apologize to you for not having been enough, for being a source of worry and disappointment, shame, anger, and anything else I might have caused you.

The need has to be clear enough to me today as I stand here, to be forgiven and to move on, to stop reacting to behavior, as a way of being. That's all I've been doing. Maybe that's why the shock was so great - at the rate I was going, muddling through on my own, I might have ended up truly helpless and destitute, homeless, like you said I might, after your death, mom.

So sorry you thought that, so sorry you told me you thought that, so sorry some part of me believed it so deeply that I created circumstances that might have led to that fate. Maybe, in my own way, I just wanted you to be right about me, mom, like moms should be right about their kids. Yet, there is still a good chance that I will recover fully now.

How much came from the fear of not being able to keep things from you? Has that been part of the paranoia? Maybe it just helped it along. Certainly for a long time I thought I couldn't shield my thoughts from you. Could you really read them, like you said, or was that part of the game? Domination worked. Did you hope to have me do things you wanted me to do, that way? Either way, with your death there is this void. It stands to reason that being dead you can no longer read my thoughts, if you ever could, but it is up to me to unlearn the habit of trying to hide.

Like my therapist said, I am not a failure simply because there is an imbalance in my nervous system when I go without medication. I live with a potential imbalance - I am not that imbalance. But I have withdrawn so much that it's hard to conceive of a real social structure. Somehow it will come, though. Only this time I will not furtively tell myself that I'm actually worthless if people know and accept me as bipolar.

This time, with acceptance coming first, with erroneous thoughts checked for my sake, not for the sake of how it looks in the family, there is likely to be a sustainable positive change. Until now, any positive change went toward restoration of the family name, of an image of myself before the failure I'd turned into, by being diagnosed as bipolar.

Slowly things will normalize: I will sleep a little less, I will get outside to walk and swim when it gets warm out, I will remember my body in its strength one muscle at a time. What I talked about today in group can actually happen: if the mind gets opposing signals, like "you have to pick up this chair" but also "you're too weak to pick up this chair," the body fumbles. It's much the same with other needs to move or change things: I've been telling myself I need a job, but at the same time I've been saying to myself that I'm ill-qualified to get one, which has led to added anxiety and no job.

I would do well to have a job for social reasons as well as for financial ones, working to chip away at the isolation I've created. I've gotten very good at sabotaging myself over the years. Without delusional thinking about my presumed contribution to the fate of the world it will be easier. And to think that it was all a way to make myself feel important, since I felt I wasn't.

This brings it further back, to college, when I chose to stay in school because my parents insisted. Words are choices too, and it's strange now to say that I chose to stay, when I felt I needed to obey. Less than a year later, I graduated and had my first manic episode at the same time, exhausting myself in the process. My reaction then was that I can't be bipolar.

Ever since, I've depended financially on my parents, first on both of them, then just on my mother. The money I earned on my own was never enough; my mother reminded me of that on a regular basis. The current result is that I'm terrified at the thought of an unstable future not too long from now, although my instincts, to preserve, to pay off debts, and to live frugally, were the ones to kick in.

Writing is worthwhile, maybe even more than before, because success is no longer the absolution from failure I'd hoped for. This fits in with the fact that the one thing that was supposed to count in my family was financial success. In the past that made me a failure. My old mumbling self is still hung up on this point, as if I'm doomed to be misunderstood.

On the one hand I've failed in the family for not "making it", on the other hand I'm in a real predicament now, isolated and low on long-term funds. Looking at writing from this point of view makes it a waste of time, since the process is ignored. I have to back away from this approach slowly, so as to not get caught up in my own web.

Writing has helped me to dig into all the corners I've fit into, some that I can only access through past writing now. The impulse to write has been a healthy one, in that it's given me distance from my situation time and again when nothing else could. Maybe it's time to allow for some success with it now, as long as it isn't the aim. Not a manic success, straight to the top, but a slow steady one, allowing for the reality of bipolar disorder which until now I've only been embarrassed about.

If I am not a failure, what am I? Let's start off with: Can it be that I'm not a failure? My work record on paper doesn't look good. I couldn't or wouldn't stick with much for very long, even though the jobs I picked were not hard. Does that make me a failure? Or does it make me a successful saboteur, instead? More likely the second: I entered situations which I quickly pooh-poohed, much like my family did, saying they were below me, if they said anything at all.

When my family said I was the black sheep of the family, as far back as '92, it stuck, and I've done black sheep things, much as people do. Now, with both old sheep dead and my sister seemingly non-descript for lack of contact, it is conceivable to be acceptable. But the reality remains that I need to shape up.

My little wild cat didn't give up on herself. That's why I had to adopt her when Josie, my old cat, died. She had lived in Mr.Greulich's basement for five years. I also still needed to take care of someone. She is smart enough to be trouble, just like me, then she worries about the trouble she's caused, just like me, but is also loving, just like me. Having committed no major crime since no major crime would occur to her, like it wouldn't to me, she commits minor ones. Since all is relative, I can say that confidently. That bit of mischief in her is much the same in me, and I wish I could console myself as much as I would console her. This is the final piece of the puzzle, the last number to the combination of the safe. The need for defiance is over.

The Little One puts up with the other two cats, who came six month later, but by reflex she is still insecure, much as I am. Yet that is what needs to turn the key, the letting go of the insecurity. When I wrote years ago about waiting to be pulverized by a fist that might have come down hard on me, I wasn't kidding. I guess I've been wincing for a long time, looking over my shoulder, waiting for that fist to come crushing down on me. Now, with even the remote possibility of that gone, I am left, much like the little wild one, with no reason to rebel, though my cat chooses to see reason still in the mere presence of the other two cats like I continued to see the same kind of need to maintain old patterns in the presence of both my parents. I was fighting windmills as a way of life, to the point of other ways being unimaginable.

Even a cat can be insecure in the way I have been, choosing to provoke in ways known in the past to bring negative consequences, like I used to say about my mother toward the end, that she needed to take a bite out of anybody just to remember that she was still alive. My response to that has been to do things that merited, in my mind, punishment, the final and total obliteration that had been promised long ago, of financial ruin.

While still on my first ward, I was told by my family that no man would want me anymore, no boss would hire me, no one would have me as a friend. It came across like a solemn promise. Before my mother's death I'd gotten very good at escaping that bite she might take out of me, but I knew only the game of forever being on the lookout for it. For my wild cat, with plenty of compassion, there's just the trap of her own behavior without punishment, so she tortures herself, not unlike I used to. In time I hope we can both forgive ourselves, for living as best we can.

Easy does it now. I'm at the hospital out-patient center again. I have associated so much harm with the hospital in the past, due to my mother's involvement in my stays here. Did it finally have to turn around for the better here, in this particular setting, across the street from the old dungeon? Maybe so, a place of so much pain finally leading to healing. On yet another day at home, looking out the window at the snow coming down, I think about what my therapist said yesterday about shifting behavior consciously, today and every day, gently. There needs to be a lot of forgiveness and healing before the job, even, so that gains can stabilize.

I have cleaned the living room and kitchen and, sitting here, I see the need for calm progress in my life, with less anxiety. The medication has stepped in to create an emotional shield. I wouldn't have been ready to start a job just now, which may sound like a copout but it isn't. The impulse to be instantly validated was an old one, and if I had gotten either of the two jobs I tried for I would have had to follow through prematurely.

A bit more nurturing is bound to help. I have some time to get my life together and I will spend it more cautiously. There will be a job when the time is right. For now, home is the key: feeling more at ease being at home, easing out of the prolonged fear of being monitored, of having my thoughts read by my mother. Time to ease out of the fear of acting, or not acting, because it might endanger people I care about if I did either.

I don't know why this thought crept in so effectively. Maybe it was just repetition, and occasional similarities in events, part of the manic pattern for me, to be sure. My mother won the battle, but since the war is over it's time to go back carefully over the impending sense of what could go wrong, as I start to remove some of the protective mechanisms which have become rigid over time.

It came up yesterday that maybe some of the protective mechanisms in place, regarding my mother, needed to be there, that they were the only way I knew to survive. So a lot of forgiveness needs to come into play here. My mother loved me in the only way that was left to her, through abuse, by dragging me into her patterns of hurt with her. With the final struggle of my non-compliance came her death, and a derailment for me. Maybe the fist did come down on me after all.

My mother lived alongside me, even from far away, and now the lack of her is what is striking. I am more than the role I have taken on since my twenties, of failure, so that she could walk alongside me over time and not feel completely excluded. Was my role all this time to dilute whatever ill I felt she was capable of? In today's light, that is the assumption. But at what cost! A quarter century of ingrained behavior to let go of now, since there's nothing left to prove. So be it. Gently now, with as much calm as possible.

Could it be that I couldn't accept shame, just like my parents couldn't, only differently? I'm beginning to believe it. Getting away from shame brought my parents to the U.S., then I shamed them by breaking down, and stayed a continuous source of shame until my mother's death. Sorry, mom, dad. Your own patched-up selves managed to get over here and have some success, but I couldn't hold the line as you might have wanted me to.

The shame you felt at my breakdown was real, and you let me feel it; I swallowed it whole and made it my own. Now it is time to filter it out from the many nooks and crannies it has settled into. The receptors for shame are now part of my makeup. As I start to give them something other than shame to process, there is a jarring reaction of chemical confusion that brings on anxiety. After all, the sludge I used to supply stayed functional for so long. Always at a loss, like the old car I once had in Alberta that needed so much oil, but at least familiar.

I used to talk to others about our needing not to live like refugees in our own lives; I even watched for that approach in the lives of others as a warning. But being spontaneous and generous to myself and others always came at a loss, in the sense that it usually came at my mother's expense. As if, if I had to put up with being the family failure, the least the family could do was splurge on me. In this sense, I was the spoiled brat my mother complained about.

Now I am my own family, with just enough money left to set up a solid first step, after paying off my debts. It will have to do, and it will. I feel no ill will there, just some anxiety related to a weak resume and low self-esteem. There is enough to work with; that is what matters.

It is just good to write again. Throughout these twenty-six years of shame, there have been positive coping mechanisms too, writing most of all. When I stopped having lithium prescribed by my old doctor, I stopped writing too, as if for fear of being found out. Now that I've been found out and reintroduced to a healthy pattern, I can have this healthy outlet back.

What made me not get another doctor to prescribe my medication right away? Was I waiting for my mother to die? Can I say that in so many words? Was subversion part of my coping mechanism? I can see that it was. But at what cost, once again: a life wrapped around another life, always referring to the other. That has been my way. Only now I can't wrap myself around a void. Being a filter for a void is pointless too. Thus the derailment right into the hospital, the reintroduction to medication, all clearly seen as positive intervention. As if an outline that had been available all along was finally adopted.

I insisted on the American option, and here I am, getting help. Will the American way hold? Will my own American dream, of becoming rehabilitated enough to work and live comfortably, happen? The storm outside is real, this late in the winter season, as was my mother's death. I will wait until it has stopped, to shovel, this time. It's already midday. A few days ago I shoveled more than I needed to and strained my left hip. This time I need to take it easy so I can work tomorrow night.

Before I decided to apply only to art schools, in my senior year in high school, before Nonna died that summer, I was following a more predictable course. After she died, thirty years ago, I became the maverick in the family. Art school was my first windmill.

Nonna came to see me at the camp I worked in that summer, a couple of weeks before she died. I was already in a pattern of holding in stress and tiredness, not letting it show. She had my father bring her and my sister to the camp. We had a beautiful day together; there were pictures. She came to check on me. Then, on the last day of camp, she died in her sleep. That night my father ended up in the hospital from exhaustion.

Conceivably he might have died too. I prayed for him from a distance, but was later scolded for staying away the extra day. I think the fact that he recovered made me think my prayers could have some effect. Subsequently, at times, in manic states, I've felt that my mental effort attached to one thing or another could help sway the outcome to a positive one. And then, over time, my goal became just surviving my mother. The deadlock was so convoluted that surviving it was the most I could hope for. Now I have, which makes for a quiet, small marker on the side of the road that is my life.

After turning everything into a potential success of a financial or social kind but not having the strength to bring about either, here I am, back to the drawing board with an able body, a little bent with a pinch of pain; a clean rug lies under my feet, there is quiet in the apartment for now, with only slight apprehension about the inches piling up on the cars, including mine, slight apprehension too about money that will need to be used carefully over the next year. Slight nervousness at soon having to handle my mother's estate here in the U.S., at my sister's request. I feel able. It is just the novelty of it that makes me nervous.

This winter, with such cold temperatures, I've stayed inside. In fact I stayed inside most of last summer too, and last fall. With the spring, I will shift my pattern to walking outdoors as soon as the snow melts, even in Cranford, which I've avoided doing. I've avoided a lot of things. I waited for my mother to die before I would try to draw attention to any of my writing. I've lived in reverse. At least I will walk in Cranford again, to start. After all, I grew up in Cranford, I still need to belong somewhere, and enough time has passed for old patterns to shift.

I could turn on the news, but I'll wait. Tonight, Saturday Night Fever is on, one of my favorite movies. I learned English by translating Bee Gees songs in '79, while my sister and I were waiting to see if we would be allowed to join our parents in the U.S. With help from new friends and a couple of politicians it happened.

That summer Nonna concentrated on the smooth tear-down of our home. It wasn't until the apartment had been emptied, the car sold, and a few things had made it to Bucharest, where my grandmother lived, that a shadow of a doubt as to what might happen to us began to appear. The schools in Bucharest refused us because we were children of defectors. Nonna promptly hired a tutor to keep us busy and took us to all the necessary appointments, including to the American embassy. It was then that the foundation started to crack for me, with the uncertainty of our ever joining our parents, which lasted until just after Christmas that year.

My withdrawal from the shore last summer was not unlike the withdrawal from my home town of Constanta to Bucharest, thirty-five years ago. Some amount of doom was not far off. My mother's illness and Mr.Greulich's were developing at the same time, leading in the fall to the death of two parents in one week. Then there was my sister's insistence on my going to Romania, which I resisted. Instead, I entered further withdrawal. And then there was the mild psychosis that early morning which led to a five-day hospital stay, getting me home a week before my birthday.

There is a parallel there, even if so many years have passed. An end of sorts then, and now. Though a beginning then and now, too. I say an end of sorts, then, because my parents seemed stressed and much too serious when we finally did join them. Their lives had entered a heavy cycle of medical exams, then internships, before they could work as doctors again. They needed all their energy, my father at fifty, my mother at forty-three, to get through the next few years. And even though Nonna came six months after my sister and I did, the strain never left. Their dreams turned out to be all hard work and no relief.

Today, on a snowy day in March, when I think of my mother I see how broken up she was when Nonna died suddenly, though very peacefully in '84. After that, there was only work to sustain her sense of worth. How difficult it must have been to trudge through so much living with my father, whom she had come to despise. When I didn't choose to join her in her attitude, and then left altogether for Montana, then Canada, she was only more isolated, with my sister already living in Europe.

So was this fall a tribute to my mother's hardship, in my own bent way? Had I come to identify myself with her that much? But then, how is it I'm still alive, when she's dead? Did some part of me make a pact, along the way, to check in alongside her, to be there as her antagonist, since I wouldn't be allowed to be anything else? Did I see it as necessary to carry the whole show to an end? Maybe so. Does that mean that on this snowy, stormy day thirty years after Nonna's death I get to start over again too, but this time in a way that is sustainable, not simply a continuation of my mother's pain?

I started writing again days ago in the form of a letter to you, mother. I will address you again today, and say: Please be glad for me now, wherever you are; own whatever is left of the heaviness I've carried for you all these years. Please, mother, take your leave in peace. Be well in the beyond, now that you are no longer constrained to your body and your pain and your anger and your sorrow. Take leave of me and be well.

Thank you for all you have given me, good and bad, and let's leave it at that. Please don't torture me anymore with the dreams you had for my success and failure. You have taught me all the lessons I am going to learn from you. Be well. Goodbye. I am starting over, almost as old as dad was when he started over with so little. Maybe I will be lucky too. I don't have friends to find me a job but I may have just enough help to get to where I need to. God bless you mom, sorry life wasn't better for you, sorry I let you down. I loved you. I tried.

It occurs to me that I've adopted a fatalistic attitude for a very long time, which I may be able to let go of, finally. I'm thinking of back in '98, when my mother had me hospitalized for a weekend and had me forfeit my stay in Canada as a result. I entered a very deep sense of failure then, aside from feeling that I failed my family and myself by being bipolar. In my mind, with my mother winning that battle, I became her lackey. It's been a long time since I've thought of it.

My sense of self was demolished. I collapsed, and for Christmas '99 I was in the hospital again, going into kidney failure from too much Haldol. I didn't die though. And I know why - I had already met my therapist at the time; his concern was the glimmer of hope that made me not give up in that basement of my parents'. The cat I had then had feline leukemia. She died instead. But with my therapist's help I got back on my feet, back to survival level. And there I've been, surviving. That gives me hope now. I can write to survive, I can work at a supermarket job if I get one, or at any other job that I get, keep doing some massage for a living, and let myself regenerate.

It's strange that it would be comforting to remember moments of pain as passages to an improved state, at this time. Today I went on two walks and spent time in two libraries, trusting in the process. After a weekend of stagnation it felt great to be outside, without pushing into a new phase, just being ready for it. Whatever comes next, something has budged.

It was striking on the way to the Roselle Park library on foot how daunted I felt, physically, despite the beautiful day. On the one hand it makes perfect sense to apply for a job at a supermarket, since I have no work experience to speak of, other than massage and a little reception work. On the other hand, the rush of embarrassment came up with the "could have done better than that" expectation. And yet, there was a computer terminal free at the library; I sat down to it for about forty minutes, filling out the online application, having already told myself that *symptoms lose their validity with daily contradiction*. It had become necessary to come up with that, as I walked, since my muscles almost balked at having that be the purpose my walk. I couldn't help but notice that my impulse to give up was as real as that. But I didn't give up.

Any work can be meditative in the end, including in a supermarket, and I badly need to work. So I kept walking, and got through the whole application. I will face my symptoms again as I apply for other jobs. Because, in the end, taking any job at all is below me, if I think along the lines of my old tape: "I will never be a doctor, so will never equal my mother, so I've lost, etc." That was the idea in '98.

But if that's true, then what's the point of my living at all? Could there be the assumption, that only by being dead would I stop being an embarrassment? Some part of me never saw that before. Did some part of my mother need me to die, and was I doing everything short of fulfilling her wish, by being such a good screw-up, a saboteur? Has this been a game with myself too, being so broken up and hurt back in '98 that I would have given in? Luckily there was the other, sturdier Canadian part of me that got me through the time in New York on my return, and then carried me, until that first glimmer of hope came.

No wonder I'm encouraged now, because it means that the sturdier part of me never left. Because when I thought "below me" on my walk through Roselle Park I was immediately able to call up thoughts of Nonna, and what came up was how she survived and carried the family to safety when her husband was jailed for political reasons. She had no problem taking whatever work was available, and they survived. She went from a comfortable upper middle class existence to being homeless and penniless overnight, with two kids and an elderly mother in tow, and adjusted.

Could I be my version of being that tough, now that I need to be, and drop any hang-ups as they come? I believe I can, though at every turn I get the tape of "such a shame, so much talent and now look at her," before I've even started working. It is key to remember that the tape player itself will work only so long as it is not stood up to, daily, with the positive insistence on doing, rather than stagnating. The heartening realization is that there is still something in me that had a respite in Canada and got strong, something positive which wants to live and will carry me to the next stage of my life.

I had a good session today with my therapist. She brings it down to Earth. I mentioned to her how afraid I've been to read, as well as write. It is surprising to find how much I am still truly afraid of my mother's power. It's good that my therapist pointed out to call up Nonna as often as I need to, because Nonna's positive presence will always be stronger than my mother's.

Now, just after five, having done my first 'thought journal', I feel more at ease. We talked about how behavior can change even after thirty years of ingrained patterns. I will print the letter to my mother with the final corrections and let it go at that. It's time to move on to this shift for the better. Tomorrow is the seminar I'm taking for continuing ed credits, on how to calm an overactive brain. The information that will wash over me then will likely fall right into place. Maybe in time it really will turn out okay.

The other thing my therapist mentioned was to think of myself as a friend I might want to help. So what would I want to say? First thing that comes to mind is to have patience. I have so little of it with myself, though I need it so badly. Listening to the cars passing in the rain outside is comforting on the one hand, but an anxious thought comes up soon after: all those people are going somewhere, and here I am stuck in my apartment with no prospects for the future. How to unlearn that, then?

First, remember the comfort part. Where does that come from? Somewhere in the past, not identifiable at the moment, but definitely somewhere in the past. Something good must have happened in the past at one point. Maybe rain, as a passage of time, can be positive again. Second, trust in the automatic movement of pencil across paper to loosen up or potentially dislodge some of the anxiety that has held on this past month. I was able to function, go to group, see my therapist, come home, feed the cats, and myself, talk politely to the lawyer about the probate issue, go see Roy, clear up an investment question with his help; then give him his massage, then find the FedEx box with some help, drop off the envelope, do cat food shopping, then come home. I also paid two bills. More than good enough.

Sitting here in my chair peacefully, I have found a little patience after all. If patience finds its way into my process more, that's a good thing. I do need to be kind to myself, even when anxious thoughts present themselves at the very mention of it. I can be kinder to myself. That is a good start. The sound of cars moving over the wet pavement is comforting.

The automatic thought I had today as I got ready, and then drove to the seminar, was that if I insisted on coming here instead of staying home someone would have to die in exchange, somewhere in the world. I can't tell how far back that goes, but the thought was familiar, and it is causing me some anxiety again. No wonder it's hard for me to function if anything

I may do can cause random people to die, in my mind. It's intense, and I need to get past it if I'm going to function fully.

This is the way in which my brain is overactive. Take it easy now, all will come, unlearning will happen. After all, now with medication, the delusion of over-importance is a memory. And today is a course on memories, in part. Something good is bound to happen. My delusions managed to settle in as fact, in the past, and it will take some time to dislodge them. This is the beginning of something.

I'll start with minimal expectations: just get through the day. *Symptoms lose their validity with daily contradiction.* The beginning of a long unwinding has to start someplace. A beginning, in this case, is an event. Fear of the future now makes sense in a new way: if I thought my every action affected the fate of multiple people, no wonder my actions were stunted. No wonder I had to limit my actions so much over the past year.

How did it get this bad, and how to make it unwind?

I have backed away so much from normal ways of doing things. I must start by letting time pass while I do things I've done off medication, like this seminar today compared to one a year and a half ago, convincing myself in this way that I'm not a danger to society, or on an undercover mission. This ties in with another automatic thought, of my life as a movie. People standing in for actors who may have had roles in other productions. Action unfolding from moment to moment.

My memory may be functioning parallel to the world I've imagined, a world in which I could be important to significant events. Taking psychiatric drugs has made for a shift in the way I recall my memories, taking them out of the spotlight and letting them settle.

As I thought, information washes over me. There is a correlation between my stunted ability to take notes and the fight to overcome the initial superstition this morning. It all ties together. I've created a linked universe in which mostly everything is 'superstition'. A lot to unlearn, letting go of my mother.

A frequent 'automatic thought' for me is that someone may have figured out there's something wrong with me, and that they'll know I'm bipolar, and if they know I'm bipolar they won't want me. This goes back to my family's comments during my first hospitalization. So, according to the 'reward theory' as I understand it, of making things more automatic, I should do something to speed the process along, of being discovered as a fraud, of being invalidated.

What I have to introduce are reminders of the fact that, although I am bipolar, I have accomplished a lot, and people do want to know me, most of all when I am the pleasant, calm person I usually am, instead of always interjecting "but wait, you just don't know how awful I really am." This is where the self-determining factor of turning love inward comes in. The more I can do that, the sooner the shift will come.

Like my therapist said, I need to think of myself as of a good friend, one who needs help rather than more battering. So, every time the "but" comes up, substitute Nonna's warmth. That straightforward. I have peace of mind that I have already proven myself enough to Nonna, that she would be or is proud of me right now, without my having to add or take away anything. With that, being bipolar can be one of my details, not the whole story. That is the shift to aim for.

In the past two months, being bipolar has been the whole story all over again, maybe even more so because of the clear need for acceptance, which is new. Since that is finally coming, and since all details are coming up bright and overwhelming, it is alright to move forward gently. It's time to see that part of me as valid and important, to acknowledge all the efforts I've made along the way to exist and survive.

I feel that my mother was always ready to invalidate me as a fraud who was pretending to be well and functioning. She would remind me that I'm ill, which would leave me feeling helpless. She always thought of me as ill, in other words *in symptoms,* even when I wasn't. She needed to insist that I was ill, so she could be well. This last time when I was entering symptoms, she died. I was left with a new situation: the dialogue became a monologue.

To face my fears now, I would have to hope that through writing I will help myself dislodge the confusion about what my mother knew: she knew I was bipolar, and always made it sound hopeless. But she didn't know that people, including me, can live with bipolar disorder without having episodes, or maybe she didn't want to know. That could finally put me in the "well" rather that the "ill" category. Instead, she poured out a tone of hopelessness about it whenever we spoke.

That tone has been getting filtered out in the last two months at such a rate as to create great discomfort, because what has come up alongside it is the truth that my being bipolar is okay. Medication is helping, I am helping myself as much as I can, I am facing my fears, and I am not helpless or hopeless. The jitters are fading, there is plenty of reason for hope.

So, when I have a massage appointment I will show up and do as good a job as I can; when I get an interview for a job I will show up and do as good a job as I can. Soon I will start lap swimming again, and continue walking. There is plenty of hope for me. Thank God.

Just like I tore pages out of some of my books to get rid of ISBN numbers, I damaged myself by not taking my medication and by having to come to a screeching halt. But the bulk of the books, even the damaged ones, are intact in the sense of their content. In a similar sense, my neurological system is essentially functional. What is going on now is the restoration of the circuits that were disrupted most, and then working inward to those less affected, and so on. So, plenty of reason to be hopeful, just like in time I may patch up all of my books again, so that in a sense they will be better than before.

Having an 'automatic thought' along the lines of "another bad day" might mean it's another bad day because mom is dead and the money might run out now that mom is dead, as if before she died there hadn't been threats that she would cut me off. There had been those, several times, but I know that it was part of how she made herself feel important; it's up to me to let that go for my own sake.

So I forgive you again, mother, and will be doing it all day as anxious thoughts come up, because you didn't know what you were doing, or that Nonna will always be a stronger presence for me. Nonna will guide me through this, by an extension of her faith. I can help myself. Since you didn't believe in God, mother, please step aside now as I construct a shield and move forward in my life.

I have been doing things in *part-acts* today, Recovery-style, dealing with high anxiety but functioning. In an hour and a half I have an hour massage to do, so I got ready, dressed in slacks and my work shirt, combed down my hair and put on a little makeup. The Kiddo is at my feet playing with a toy. The other two cats are near. The classical station is on. The yams are cooking on the stove. As I write even this much, I unwind a little. I wonder if my 'reward center' is trying to keep me from writing because writing is the bulk of the 'control mechanism' for me, other than actual massage work. Doing, the learned skill part, comes into play. When I write, it's time to slow down, by definition, especially by hand, like now.

Other than that, I dared myself to sign up for the Y today, and did it; I will dare myself now to go do laps at 8pm since there are lessons between 5 and 8pm. I went and got goggles and a lock, the last of what I needed, and will get in the car at a quarter to eight and go. I'm having to force myself to do all this, but doing it. I went to the library to delete spam emails and do a final printout for "letter to mom." I have to sustain the effort as I go. My right foot hurts a little from walking.

Coming in the door after my walk in the rain, one thought stands out: I really am alone, even in familiar surroundings. No more mom and dad, nothing but distance from my sister. And yet, since I had left the radio on, an opera is on, and the cats welcomed me as they always do. So there is something here after all. There is something to start with, as I start again. Only a little, but enough. Tomorrow morning, first thing, I will swim a little. Getting a schedule going will be useful. Also, I try to remember some humor. It has been lacking for the past two months. But the essential thing is to get past this feeling, the starkness of being alone. Massage work, sparse as it has been, will have to do for now, as I get my bearings. I have been filling up time with tasks, priming the pump for more of a real existence again. The way to a more stable bearing will have to take its time, without rushing.

The massage yesterday went well and showed good results. It felt right to be doing the work, which makes me think that I should still make more of an effort to continue, if I can, instead of working only at a regular job, if I'm able to get one. Which means getting more business cards again, and opening my mind to new clients.

The bulk of my getting better, more sure of myself, etc., will rest on replacing damaging habits with positive ones that will restore my will. Getting out in the world is part of it. So is getting more comfortable with my private world as it stands now. That includes the starkness that has been presented by the meds.

In holding up the dam to old delusions, the new meds and the medicated state itself have encountered interference. Traces of old delusions show up and the feeling is of a lack of ability to deal with reality in its starkness. Yet the delusions were just that, delusions: I never helped any of my favorite actors get through trials by watching them intently as they got through their movies. I was just watching movies. Now, for the time being, I'm not watching any movies at all. I also have no heightened agendas romantically, in the same way. Dead stop there. The control system instituted by the medication has cleared the deck.

So what was real, from before? That might be a scarier question even than "Am I entirely alone?", because I can't tell where I stopped imagining and started functioning. The need for medication is clear. What is not clear is just how deluded I was living, day to day. I was shielding people I cared about from my mother, or so I thought, and thwarting her actions in my world by denying more and more people access to me. Since this doesn't make sense to regular people just living their lives, it goes without saying that I've alienated the bulk of my clients as a result, who used to make up my social network. So now what? Rebuilding slowly is the only clear path. In the meantime, I'm working on changing old habits, being pleasant without imposing, as opportunities come up.

I take comfort in my cats. We get through the days together. It's time to *make a business of Recovery* all over again, *trigger spotting* often, and adding the new tool of 'thought journaling'. Same basic concept: *trigger symptoms require trigger spotting,* and then adding more detail to the 'automatic thought' to clarify the setting, to start to get some idea as to how to unwind these automatic thoughts, one at a time, meanwhile becoming more forgiving of myself for having gotten so lost. Which I have been. Alive but very lost in the corridors of my own imagined life, at least enough of the time to have me feel derailed, now, still.

And yet, there is nothing to be done but to walk, swim, write, show up, do things that trigger old habits, like wanting to spend time with my mother or even my sister, but not going through with old impulses. *Daring to do the things I fear to do to prove there is no danger.* This is my challenge:

walking past memories of mixed emotional baggage. With massage, the focus comes easily; swimming just started again and is more about the social aspect of health. Walking was hard today as if I had to drag myself along, but there is no getting around it. Just have to do it. Writing too. Just putting pen to paper like this, getting through the sludge and no more, at least part of the time. What I've been afraid of most as a potential situation is what I'm going through now - having to go it alone. Here I am, having to face my fears on my own, and doing it.

Today has been much better than last week, when I was in high anxiety all day, every day. It's time to endorse myself a little again. It's been a feat to do so. I just set my alarm for 6:30 tomorrow morning to go swimming. Changing patterns, literally, seems to be helping. No issue at all taking medications anymore, so that any duality as to that is gone.

It came up today that I was on a manic high when I was raped during my first manic episode, and that the trauma of the rape never got sorted out. Everything was kind of thrown together at the time, shame on top of trauma. It boomeranged in a big way on thinking of it lately. Through the rape, I found out that I could be stripped of all logical protection without warning, at a time when I was most vulnerable. With my mother's death, many parallels were drawn to that first time on a ward. On top of that there was the perceived loss of financial protection from my mother. As a result I have been feeling very exposed and vulnerable, and the trauma and circumstances of the rape were revisited very strongly.

Today I made it to the pool in the morning, went to church, went for a walk and just came back from checking on the grieving seminar in Cranford. The next one will be in September, but in a month I can go to the open support group. I also finished typing out notes for this week. Something has shifted. The sense of being alone is not quite as overwhelming, and I'm hoping for better sleep tonight, feeling tired already.

What struck me in my notes, before my walk this afternoon, was how much letting go I must still do, of my mother. She was the hopeless one, in ways, the one to feel sorry for. And I did feel sorry for her, these past thirty years. I just didn't realize how much. I felt so sorry for her that I adopted some of her ways of *helplessness* and *hopelessness.*

Throughout, I defied my mother at my own peril. Some part of me insisted that I wasn't bipolar, so that I couldn't be the hopeless creature she always brought up. It's not so much that I believed what she was saying about me, it's more that I couldn't have her go it alone. A part of me shared her depression.

She used to say that she was depressed "for real reasons." Aside from medicating herself, she never addressed depression as such in an accepting way. It makes sense that she had to think of me as ill to think of herself as well.

The pang of depression coming in from the swim this morning was real and intense, though, all for me. Weeks ago I would have thought my mother was living through me, while the feeling lasted, and a great hopelessness would compound through the day. Today I *spotted* right away that especially when dealing with automatic thoughts of this strength *I should be occupied rather than preoccupied.* So I went right away to give myself the pedicure I needed; then I realized that part of the depression had come by checking the mail and finding the power bill there, with the same trigger of "money slipping away" that I've felt before. So I decided to distract myself more by planning to go to church, which I did although I felt uncomfortable throughout. I had to dare myself to bear the discomfort of being in public, and got through it. Then I came home and laid down. I couldn't really sleep,

18

but rested, with two of the cats. Then I had lunch and typed up notes. It all felt a little less forced.

The break of the day came with that insight about my mother, before my walk. How intertwined our lives had been. For thirty years, since Nonna's death, she had me to intertwine with, all the time telling me that she could read my thoughts, knew what I was doing, etc. On my walk, I felt that she was actually the hopeless one all along, and I had no trouble finding energy despite the wind and the cold. Yesterday I had been dragging myself around. Now I know, if another crushing 'automatic thought' of helplessness comes in, to immediately divert my attention to any task rather than wallow in the feeling.

Just now I hit a real slump. The bill for the labwork related to the doctor's visit came in the mail today and I called my insurance company to see if my insurance is still active and would cover it. Yes to both. I was relieved, but there is a basic issue here - I have never fully supported myself and now I'm hardly working, on top of it. Money will run out eventually, even though this bill is paid. Soon, now, God-willing, I will make that turnaround that grants me security, or a sense of security, for the first time in my life.

I have felt insecure for thirty years. I have limped along with mom's financial help for the last fifteen. Would that God grant me the opportunity to finally thrive in the light. Nonna, please help. I don't know what to do. I paid the rent for next month this morning, and the power bill, bought the new work shoes I needed and two pairs of pants at the thrift store, ordered more business cards, swam, walked, and rested in between. It's getting nice out. And yet, there is this depressed feeling as if time and money are running out. I don't know whom to ask for help, except for Nonna and God.

Tomorrow is a day for groups. There is a sinking feeling there too. I need them more than I would like to think. Who will take care of me? Why does that still come up? I have to calm down and get a job, but the dependence habit comes up strong. It will have to let it run its course on its own. I've come to a dead end, that's all, I'm in helpless mode again. And yet there's more.

Drudgery is to be expected. After thirty years of lacking, no wonder there's another slump. I want to do something about my writing in the way of promoting it, but dare not think of spending money on it. If it did take off, would that be okay? Yes, at least that. It would be okay now for people to know about my being bipolar. Finally. After so long. It would be okay to have them see that. Maybe that's all that's got me down. I should make an investment of a few hundred dollars and see what happens. Why is it so painful to have something to promote? Still having trouble with what I'm promoting?

The 'automatic thought' that comes up is that it's a waste of time, but since my mood has already lifted I will now spend some time going through with what I'd promised myself to do - promote my writing after my mother's death. If not now when, as the saying goes. There will be options to choose from and it is something I should do, since so much of my life is writing, since writing helps me get along.

Thank you God, and Nonna. It makes everything easier to bear, to have something to look forward to. I will have tried, if nothing else. I owe myself that. And the last of it is happening right in this apartment, which has gone through so many changes with me. Why not? At least try. It's that straight-forward, though I know I will have symptoms along the way, maybe even like the intense ones today, chipping away at the big picture.

P~art~ T~wo~

R~eviewing~ and previewing are favorite pastimes of the nervous patient. *I* have spent time writing so I could make sense of my life. I have reviewed and, in hoping for a better future, I have previewed. Enough said now. What's left to do is to return to what's already down on paper, gingerly, to see past the process, to allow meaning to emerge at whatever rate is suitable.

What would I write about now, compared to years ago? I've lost the drive, the need to prove myself sane. I was sane, for a long stretch, up to my mother's death last year. Then I imploded, and I'm still finding my way, with the help of a therapist and a psychiatrist. Sometimes fear overcomes logic, again. Am I still the big car that thinks it's a little car?

I went back to doing massage work this summer, until my knee almost gave out a month ago. I've been feeling withdrawn again, for the lack of swimming and walking. This spring, writing took me into the stream of 'negative core beliefs', so I've been hesitant to get back into it. For today, this notebook is what there is.

The Little One is gone now. I had her put down the first week of August. This spring, in my "letter to mom," I had written about her being always on edge due to her overactive thyroid. She would poop outside the box and expect to be punished for being unpleasant or sick. In June she started also peeing outside the box, and became frantic to go in and out of our apartment into the hallway, meowing by the door, eating double and then triple the amount of food she used to, but not finding any relief. I decided not to go with the medicine that is available because it seemed to me that her quality of life would have diminished even more, if I did. Now, in the first week of October, almost two months since having her put down, I find harmony again in my home with the other two cats.

My book LIKE NEW feels right, upon reading it again. Last week I made some corrections to it. It's whole even as it is, I was glad to see. It holds up. Still, it strikes me that I am more stable now than I was toward the end of it, although then I had steady work and my old cat Josie, whom I loved very much. I was sure, then, in my defiance of the medical profession. I took my medication and followed the rules, yet questioned being bipolar. The diagnosis had seemed like punishment for twenty years.

When, with my mother's death, I crashed and ended up in the hospital again in January, I had to finally look at it differently. My mother had left a great void, and I had only been taking a naturopathic mood stabilizer instead of lithium, for over a year. I managed the best I could for two months after she died, but entered a psychotic state the early morning I was taken to the hospital. A month later, after a quick release and more denial on my part, I started my recovery in earnest through the out-patient program. I had stayed out of the hospital for thirteen years, had managed, but it wasn't enough.

This time, with the right help, I am coming into acceptance in a way I couldn't have before, now that I can't blame my mother for my illness anymore, since she's dead. We're done struggling with each other, and it has made a difference. There's just me.

More than likely, I will have to shift to other work, having come to understand that my massage work filled in as my social life in a way that wasn't necessarily helpful. Going through the grief seminar now, I realize the need to change that. I need more than glimpses of friendship through service. I need what I haven't had before, a balanced life.

Having to deal with pain in old injury sites, physically, makes me see that massage was at least in part about instant gratification, which came almost every time. That used to get me past the strain of the actual work. I felt needed, worthy; it gave me a purpose. It gave me a shield against my mother.

I turned off my cell phone the weekend she died, thinking she was going to be released from the hospital, since she seemed to be improving. With the news of her death, what was left of my shield fell to pieces, not to be mended. I tried to keep working, but found it difficult to continue. I sent out refunds to clients who had bought packages and waited for the fist to come crashing down on me, finally, and this time it did. What still strikes me as odd is that I am now recovering. Thinking that I've never made money at anything but massage, I'm scared. Yet the shift needs to come. It's always felt strange taking money for healing work anyway; it feels even more so now.

Financially, I have time to get myself together, and that allows me to take physical warnings seriously. My pattern of caregiver must shift or even be allowed to die out. That makes for more insecurity, but since it's what needs to happen I must go through with the process. A part time job for the sake of socialization, rather than a career in massage therapy, makes more and more sense.

I've told myself time and again that if only my mother weren't there to criticize, I wouldn't be bipolar. I would do very well financially, in general, and with massage work in particular. Now I am having to reconsider my need for success, since the drive to succeed in itself is part of the old pattern, one which I must leave behind. I didn't work to make a living, I worked to prove that I'm a regular person, free of mental illness, who could belong, like anyone else. Being bipolar and belonging seemed a contradiction of terms.

As I am still in the early stages of recovery, after so many years, with acceptance as my focus, I must give myself time now. Kindly, I must let go of the great secret hope that it was all a mistake, that I wasn't bipolar after all. Whatever financial success I had was based on that belief. I worked hard, like the regular person I wanted to be, and got paid. My challenge now lies in accepting that I can be bipolar and earn a living at the same time. But being bipolar still means failure for now, thus is a contradiction of terms when it comes to money.

I didn't get the emotional support I needed in the family, and now with both parents dead and an estranged sister, I never will. My mother's financial help, without the emotional component, only reinforced my sense of failure. The revelation, this year, that the support I need can come from elsewhere, is as painful as anything else.

From the point of view of needing to build a new plateau to stand on, my book LIKE NEW might not seem to pertain to me anymore, but it does. The 'daring to exist' through writing back then was what kept me alive. I was doing the best I could with what was available to me. Even publishing my writing online was a feat, though I couldn't go one more step and promote it. I was documenting what came, as it came, as a way of creating a marker that couldn't be erased. All my other creative work had gone by the wayside, and massage was always to be experienced only in the present moment. Only writing, in my experience, could have held. And I believe that my book has held, seeing how it helps me to accept myself now. In time, I hope it will do the same for others.

When I would deny my worth again, as I have in the past, the writing will be there to get in the way, to suggest more. Writing has been part of the process of grieving, for so much that I haven't been able to grieve for in other ways. In helping me to find a new footing, it has already fulfilled its goal. Since being bipolar always meant failure, in my family, I worried a lot about being found out as one. I've lived in hiding for a long time. The challenge to disentangle myself from that pattern continues.

One of my mother's needs while she was alive was to have me found out. Each time I failed, in each way, I became needy again for her intervention. She needed that badly to be needed. No matter how sad that is, it is a truth to be faced, as is the need to forgive her and myself before going on. It's little wonder, then, that I couldn't accept being bipolar, and that the shift to acceptance is difficult. To have gone from helplessness implied in all my actions and with only temporary gains, to a more sustainable sense of belonging, is already a big step.

A long time ago, Tyler said that I'm an immigrant who should be glad just to have a roof over her head. That had a powerful effect, and although I'm over it now I will not be able to erase the thought entirely from my mind. Since what I need most, still, is to feel like I belong, somewhere, I need to allow time to heal what wounds that are still open, as far back as being uprooted thirty-six years ago. The answer to "Am I still a refugee, inwardly, after all these years?" is yes. I've had the "beggars can't be choosers" attitude in my relationships, after that initial break at twelve. Can I cut myself a new path now, as an adult? I need to, so the answer must be yes to that too . What will it take?

Certainly, I have to "take myself off the clearance rack." The way I know I'm still there is that I continue to look for quality on actual clearance racks or at the thrift store I go to, since I trust in my ability to find Quality anywhere. I find confirmation there, each time, that things of quality, slightly used, are still worthwhile, so that maybe I am too.

In the past, putting myself on the clearance rack was also a way of testing the buyer. If they didn't see the diamond in the rough, so to speak, it was easy for me to pass judgement on them, in any essential way. I hid my own essence from them and moved on. But this translates also into being unable to accept help, always seeing an implied debt. This came from what I felt I owed my parents, and could never repay; it will take some time to see being on display at all as a valuable part of life. "Putting oneself out there" still seems dangerous, though it needn't be.

Maybe I gave up competing for men too early on, after my sister's taking on the first guy I fell for, at sixteen. Fate soon provided his best friend, whose affection I will never forget. My mother made a point of driving him away. After that no one she ever got wind of survived as a partner for me, so I took to hiding wherever I could in that sense too, not in the least on the clearance rack. I didn't want my men destroyed by my family's attention.

Am I still hiding now, almost a year after my mother's death? I know that the answer is yes, because when my sister let me know this week that she'll be in New York next week, and would like to see me, the first thing I thought of was that I didn't have a boyfriend to show off to her. And yet, my second thought was that I wouldn't have wanted my sister to meet him anyway, if I had one, because part of me still sees her as a threat in that respect. Having a boyfriend would prove to her that I am not a failure, but at the same time it might damage him. So I will meet her and my niece on my own, after a pause of eight years. That will have to do. It should be alright for me to have more confidence in myself by now, but since I'm not there yet, I need to give myself more time there in that aspect also.

This shift on all fronts is a challenge alright, as it turns out. I lost my mother, Mr.Greulich, and the Little One, all in less than a year, and am still grieving. When this stage is completed, I will find myself altogether elsewhere. The pattern is in the process of shifting, due to my having survived the death struggle with my mother. Now I need to find my place as an adult for the first time, finally adopting adult ways.

My concern is, am I so stuck in my old ways that someone has to forcibly take me off the clearance rack and shower me with affection, before I can truly enjoy life, or am I capable of taking myself off it, dusting myself off and then meeting someone? I've been a caregiver for others, now I need to look after myself. It's an old question, but the answer is still the same. First-borns are only comfortable with buying new, I've been told, while younger siblings such as I was make do with hand-me-downs. There must be a compromise there somewhere, now that I shouldn't have to hide any prospective lover any more.

I manage without a social structure, but just barely. My current isolation at home with my cats has proven as much. Though I wouldn't want anyone to be everything to me all at once, to fill my space with their world and their life so that I could just ignore the emptiness in mine, I do see the need for companionship at the deep level that leads to love, or is part of it. Managing is not enough, not the same. The one time when it might have worked out from the start I was too afraid of my parents' wrecking our happiness. Now it's time to stop thinking that way. But where to start? Definitely not online. I feel so isolated that I can only hope that fate will take a hand, again. Can it be that simple, like a trickle turning into a stream as soon as the surroundings allow for it? I certainly hope so. Not so much a miracle, as a natural progression.

Meanwhile writing helps, again, with that little bit of distance it creates, which is so necessary. Fear recedes again, with the 'daring to exist.' It's my way of getting grounded. Maybe more than that. With one cat at my feet and the other one nearby, my home and my self are lit from within, tonight. It has come through faith in what is, in myself and in the process of healing. Tomorrow is another day to start again. With any fears that will come, this well-being will have stayed.

On the first anniversary of my mother's death I am reminded of another loss, an older one, on leaving Romania for the first time. Yesterday I watched a movie I already knew, but this time I cried so hard through it and afterward that today I still have a left-over headache. As I prepare myself for the day, I look for a way to function despite the deep sense of loss. I am thinking of the moment at the airport in Bucharest, when the time came to go past the point of no return, to turn away from Nonna and Kiki. I thought I would never see either again. Tears came in abundance, as they did yesterday. I knew then what it was to be torn from my life. But I could see the depths love can reach at the same time; I feel as lost now, yet I draw faith from the bond of love that existed between me and my grandmother.

On that first plane ride, a woman sitting near me told me that I had reason to hope in my life to come, that I was a very lucky girl. She said that with such compassion and sincerity that it reached me. I was able to calm myself, and to get through the flight with composure. I became determined to make the best of what was to come.

It has never been as clear to me as this morning that at that time I wasn't just leaving what had been my country and my home: I was also losing Nonna, and losing her was more painful than losing my parents when they defected. Today I am convinced, more than ever, that she left her own life and her son behind six months later so that she could be there for me. She did it with faith, as she did everything. She died with faith too, four years later, with a smile on her face and chocolate still in her dentures. Her life was fulfilled.

This morning, heavy with a sense of loss, it is because of Nonna's faith that I will function, go to the bank, get money out, go to the store, buy flowers and a candle and matches, and go to the cemetery to wish my mother a safe journey away from this place. It felt yesterday as if she had been hanging around this past year, that it was partly her sorrow that brought on the tears, as if I had finally set her down after still carrying her. Now I will care for her differently, and for my sister. The anger I used to feel toward them is completely gone, the last of the thorns have been pulled out, now there is just the healing that needs to take place. The compassion I felt at the grieving seminar has allowed for it.

This morning I am as if on that first flight over the Atlantic, having dried my tears, establishing a new custom of celebrating my sister's birthday and my mother's passing on the same day by lighting a candle and bringing flowers to Nonna's grave. When I get home, my cats will be there; more will happen.

Now I won't have to pretend to be happy. I can be sad for as long as it takes. I will mourn that first break and all the following losses, functioning through the process. I used to say that my mother needed to take bites out of people periodically to remember that she was still alive.

It's just occurring to me now that my need to break up my own life was not unlike that: that bringing about my own destruction, including during this past winter, was the only way I got confirmation that I was still alive, like some people need to cut their own flesh or burn it with lit cigarettes to feel something, anything. My cycle of destruction was more brutal, every time, as if it was unbearable to me to have survived my mother and father if I couldn't know love from them. I felt that love had been there but was replaced by superficiality.

I was much like my father in turning away from a social life, on coming to the States. Maybe I was just learning from him, as I had done when I was little. Since his withdrawal was what came through, and his need to dominate, that's what I did too. Now I am as alone as he was even before the Alzheimer's, but I have the chance to rebuild. The reason I know that's true is that my instincts for self-healing are in place. I am making efforts every day and every week to forgive myself, though there is still more and more pain to go through. What is more important is that I am asking for help, at the rate and in the ways in which help from others can be effective. I'm still scorched internally, but capable of faith and hope, the same kind of faith and hope as on that first plane ride. That first gaping wound can now close, letting the tough little kid that I was grow into more. I, as a member of my family, have never before been able to allow for more. My warped sense of responsibility toward my family hasn't allowed for it.

I failed my parents, only to find out now that I couldn't have done anything but. They were so damaged internally but so tough externally that their failed expectations were the only thing they could put across to me. My sister left, first to go to college and then to live in Switzerland. That I accepted as her way of coping. I assumed the role of the needy child so my parents could function, so I could get a form of love through money and through their attention when I was sick.

Then I straightened up to care for my father when he got sick, and helped my mother in the ways that I could. But in the process I spent my own energy. They accepted my help and came to depend on it, but in the end they both knew how to show love toward me only through abuse. They lived a warped version of the strictness they'd learned at home after their families had been mistreated by the communists. They spent their lives hurting each other, especially after the move to the U.S., because that's all they knew.

I spent my life first running away, then trying to "fix it," much like my parents did. First, by getting married to the first man who agreed, then by trying to make it work despite a break between us early on. I resorted to emotional violence when it became clear that my husband would always need more reassurance: I left him for another man. I'd learned abuse from my parents but used it only as a way to break myself free from unmanageable situations.

However successful the breaks were, a sense of defeat soon followed, for a simple reason: my extremely sensitive nervous system couldn't handle stress at the rate that my parents' did. My bipolar illness was more severe than their anxiety and depression had been. They had made it through mental breakdowns in their twenties by burying the damage and functioning as if from emergency to emergency. When I broke down, it was as if they had failed too. They couldn't live with that.

What I can understand now, which I couldn't before, is that I had to become something my parents needed to fix or have fixed, because otherwise they would have had to look at their own unresolved pain. That would have been unbearable to them. They both spent their lives fixing other people's lives, not in the least in their work as doctors, but there I was, resisting their effort and authority. They had to break me "for my own good." Then, when they couldn't put me back together again, they hoped I would at least stay put, first in their home, then in the home I'd made for myself as a married woman. But I wouldn't stay put. Something in me insisted on getting away from abuse, even at the risk of more damage.

So here I am this morning, one year after my mother's death, fingering my scars and wounds after burning my life to a crisp once again. This is finally my life to honor, but is it too late? Have I done too much damage, or have I allowed for too much? The answer is that I can and will be able to open myself to love that is not abusive, after all. Since the opportunity is there for recovery, I must follow through with it. The war is over. Healing can happen. I allowed my mother to die, last year at this time – I didn't go to see her as I did another time she almost died, over twenty years ago. I put myself first, and that tore me wide open. Yet surviving my mother was the right thing to do.

Now I have to continue to get better, because it makes sense, and is the only thing that makes sense. I find every day that more patience is needed, so I work on that. The brightness of the world still seems stark, but I function, which is all I need to do, for now. Many people are part of the picture, but only remotely, so I am taking it slowly. That is where faith comes in, and acceptance. Being bipolar is no longer a criminal sentence; correcting a chemical imbalance through medication is no longer a burden. I can foresee a future in which I will be useful despite my limitations, or even because of my ability to accept them.

This is the shift in 'core beliefs' that my therapist and I have talked about. It turns out that it really is as hard as getting off the highway I know by heart and cutting myself a brand new path by hand. I won't get as far, definitely won't get there as quickly, but maybe I never needed to. Writing loosely by hand again is part of that, as will be the process of editing afterward. Writing is still the tool I cut my path with. It gives me the courage I need to put on my shoes, my coat, to get ready to go out. It makes me want to park a little ways away from the bank so I can get a short walk in, to order two egg rolls from the Chinese restaurant and wait patiently for them, to go to the supermarket and get flowers, a candle, and matches. It is a beautiful sunny day out. No one will know any more about me than what they see, and they will see the same person they know, functioning. My cats accept me as I am every day, with love and compassion. The time will come to allow others to do the same. Maybe not right away, but soon. Then, things will happen differently. For now this sense of transition is what is.

Sunday afternoon. I woke up with a sense of fear and loneliness again this morning. Still no job, just the love of my two cats and the plan to continue going to my loss support group on Sunday nights. My knee still hurts, so I haven't returned to walking and swimming, after a brief attempt ten days ago.

I have a little fearful anticipation as to Thanksgiving dinner since I was invited out, and then there's the class reunion two days later. It doesn't take much to let anxiety rise. But I have become accustomed to my Wednesdays at the program within the hospital out-patient program, which always end up being helpful. I still feel stuck much of the time, but I'm able to back up and see more of the larger picture more often.

So much is about perception. On waking up, I usually have to make an effort to frame my actions within my life. I try to see them as worthwhile, even when the lack of action is all there is. It feels like the clock is ticking down to some event, like I should be doing something about it, but I don't know what or how. I can see this need only as a need for acceptance, since there isn't a particular event I am anticipating. I just have a general sense of malaise. I try to shift out of it by putting on a sobering movie, I do dishes and make the bed, I know that I will go to the support group tonight, yet it feels like there's something I'm not doing, for lack of perspective. All I can do is trust in the process.

As much as I can sometimes see myself as part of something bigger, something meaningful, as much as I can see that I have reached a place of balance from a neurological point of view, I am still afraid of losing myself again in emotional upheavals. I feel that I am part of something, and then my 'negative core beliefs' come back full speed before I can get out of the way, reminding me that I am not enough.

I feel polluted again upon waking up, as if I'd spent a whole day watching television or had a conversation with my mother, as in the past. It could be that I'm dreaming about interaction with her. The sense of helplessness is old, at least as old as my diagnosed illness, and I realize when I'm in it that it is something learned, which I must unlearn, being as sensitive as I am, before I can sustain happiness.

I am doing everything I can, staying cheerful, going out into the world here and there, now and then, I am curbing my spending while accepting my sense of inadequacy about it; I am no longer driven out of my own life or my own space by impulses which I can't resist. I allow the world around me in only a little at a time, at a rate I can handle.

The decision to no longer do massage for a living is part of that, creating a shift in the structure of my life, away from the painful need for approval. All this time alone is about finally saying to myself, not so much to others, that I am worthy of all my own efforts until I don't feel inadequate in my own life anymore, until I have healed. The Way, the Tao, has been part of me all this time, and, if I allow it, it will heal me. As it penetrates my wounds, there is the pain related to cleansing and healing, which is different from the pain incurred in just surviving.

That pain had the role of shocking me periodically out of the numbness that had become my life. I have deep wounds, internally, and each one must be anointed and healed before more is to happen. Fully accepting the scars that form as a result is as painful as the healing itself, yet only acceptance can carry a sense of being whole again.

I have been surviving for a very long time. Some of the time now I know that I belong in my own life, more often since going to the loss support group. I get the sense that help is coming, that it is active in my life, as if I am no longer fighting God by always pointing out my lacks. I have the courage to see myself as something worth more.

My cats are more direct. They lend their compassion to me outright. As I sit on the sofa in the living room, I am aware of The Kiddo right behind my head on the chest of drawers. She needs to be loved too. Being a cat, she is the one who defines the distance between us based on what she can handle. Sometimes she comes to lay on my chest or belly, sometimes Vinny comes and burrows into my side as a way of communion, and I feel whole, as I do now with The Kiddo keeping me company. She has begun to come onto the bed too, which I like. Our love for each other is getting stronger, and she is daring to show it in ways she was reluctant to, before.

There is a white cat in the parking lot that looks hungry. I fed it once. But I notice that my urge to care for it more than that has been curbed by my sense of responsibility toward my own cats. The impulse to rescue is being addressed. Feeding that cat only once in a while is a compromise I am willing to make.

I still miss The Little One, sometimes thinking that I could have done better by her, experiencing the same guilt as my guilt toward my mother. But then I remind myself of the need to live within my limitations. I remind myself that I did the best I could at the time and that I need to forgive myself for it if it was wrong. Indecision as to the Little One's fate would have made it worse. I was dealing with duality, and it was important to make a decision and follow through, for my own sake.

What is my life now? It is the process of healing. Uneasiness and discomfort come with it. I need to find a sustainable balance so that I will no longer be floored by being reminded that I'm bipolar, and by the fact that so many hurdles have cropped up in my life because of it. Since I am finally in a financially stable period, it is time to strengthen other aspects of my life which can become stable, mostly through the positive use of the passage of time. Writing turns out to be my tool, and in time it will become more and more useful. It is no longer about accomplishing things, as LIKE NEW was an attempt to clear myself of the "sentence" of being bipolar. I can now accept that that's what it was, since that kind of effort was all that kept me going, and I might not have survived without it.

On reading LIKE NEW again it becomes obvious to me that, throughout, I was still clinging to the struggle with my family in a way so old that I didn't know anything else. Everything else was secondary to this thirty-year war. I have been just surviving for a very long time. Now it's important to disentangle the positive developments along the way, from the destructive patterns that I came to know so well, and, without forgetting them, to move past them.

The Kiddo is weary of sounds outside or in the hallway of our building like I am weary of old impulses, but the question of whether I will move on and create a new life for myself has been answered: yes, I will. The reason is trust in the process of healing. God, seen as what encompasses The Way, has been present all along. The Way IS the process. Nothing is entirely outside it. No damage done, no hardships endured. It is all part of coming to the present moment and staying aware of it, as I continue moving forward. Is the world as I know it falling apart? Yes, it is. Is abuse still prevalent in so many ways? Yes. My challenge will be to find a way to move through it, with it, to flow with it in such a way as to maintain aspects of harmony within it, even when destruction might be happening all around me.

This has been a major stumbling block for me, the inability to accept injustice or inequality when I see it, as if it were my task in life to right them. It occurs to me now more clearly that the only way to acceptance is by gradually learning to sift through events, as to find out what I can help with, even if all I can do is show more tolerance. Noise of one kind or another seems to be the only way many people can interact, now, whereas for me stillness and quiet need to happen at regular intervals, if I am to function as well as I'm able.

Sleep is important for balance. I get a lot of sleep now, with the new medication. It's lucky that it's working so well. Some people never get to that point. I am able to reason and function and heal, slowly, and to look forward to more. The old underlying worry, of not being able to function at all if I accepted being bipolar, is shifting, nearly gone.

In high school and college I had wondered what happened to people when they went over the edge. For myself that question has been answered: I can make it back, I have made it back. The malaise or exhaustion related to the effort will pass. With that in mind, it's time to gently shake myself off, having fallen into the dirt, and to walk on, this time at my own pace, rather than trying to ride wild horses; to save my energy for the times I do go out, since the issue with my knee is present more than ever; to value my home, even if it is a rented apartment and not a house; to value my daily companions, my two cats; to value the heartening presence of positive thoughts, memories, ways of slowly chipping away at old barriers to well-being, since violent ways of overcoming them have proved destructive. In this way, a weekend at home becomes a gift, not an imposition. Slowly, impulsive behavior fades, and the need to act, when it comes, is appropriate.

So, again, there is the process. Filtering out destructive behavior carefully is part of it. It involves retaining a record of the way to destructive behavior, as a safeguard to returning to it when the impulse resurfaces. Since my nature has changed from so many years of abuse, this is crucial. Now, having survived my life as it has been, there is the potential in me again for wisdom not unlike Nonna's. That would be a privilege, to be able to live as an adult the attitude Nonna brought me up with, as a child. It is something to be learned and valued, not to be taken for granted. It takes effort and perseverance, and it's worth it. A relationship with a man after that will be the icing on the cake, based not on despair and neediness but on an ability to share valuable life lessons.

I need to remember to be weary of anyone who would be comfortable bleeding away at my essence in the future. It started with my father, before I had a chance to consider what was right for myself, and it has continued. Now I need to revisit the sense of loss I experienced when he died, to heal that wound too, and move on.

The need to abuse kindness or love is not irresistible, even if the path to it has been smoothed by decades of practice. This is one of those wide-eyed moments of realization for me, necessary if I'm to change future patterns for myself as a mate. I need not run into anyone's arms anymore, so as to escape my fate. I've done the best I could until now, and now I can do better.

What comes up again and again is how strange it is to have survived this pattern at all. One of my 'negative core beliefs' is that I can't do better than live in this way. It takes patient clarity to create a shift to something better, to the sense of being worthwhile. I feel polluted, damaged, and I am, but I also have the opportunity to move away from this core belief altogether. My will makes it so.

In time there may be someone who can appreciate the efforts made, someone with whom it will be possible to survive old tendencies of becoming destructive, as they resurface in either of us. Rescuing is no longer an option, if it ever was. A year after my mother's death, that is the only certainty, other than my resolve to recover.

The world has not stopped, politics and wars rage on, everything still costs money, winter is just about here; what there is for me from now on, is more of the process of healing, through standing firm when old patterns would tell me to stand down, to give up, to grovel, to abuse my resources, to act out of despair. No matter how many times and how forcefully these impulses come, driven by core beliefs, my job is to get out of their way, if I can, while still moving forward; and if I can't, to *bear with the discomfort* until they pass. To eat, to sleep, to function.

In time things will shift to where I can watch world events on television without being overwhelmed. Until that time, I will watch my own movies, turn to my own books and writing tools to get through what is too much to bear. The sense of responsibility for what is wrong in the world needs to fade.

It would have been impossible for me to enter a healthy relationship with a man before this realization, and even now I'm not quite there, but I'm close. I have been known to retreat so quickly from genuine affection as to become instantly unreachable, shifting any potential relationship to friendship, if that, otherwise retreating completely. In my mind, my retreat would at least allow both of us to survive the onslaught of critical reactions, perceived or real. Not to mention the times I've taken physical communion out of despair, only to live with the damage done by retreating within myself later.

It's something like withdrawal from a potent substance, what I'm going through now, from my mother's abusive behavior and from the drive for instant gratification, in more ways than one. In general I don't have an addictive personality, but I have experienced dependence very strongly at emotional levels. And, as is often the case, the dependence was not on a positive aspect of a relationship but on destructive behavior that was encouraged early on; in other words, what I knew as behavior.

It's lucky that Nonna was in my life throughout my childhood, because without her positive influence I wouldn't have made it. Now I see myself as one who has survived a great war, without ever having gotten the training to get through it, almost as a fluke. But I have to get myself into the proper environment for healing, as my loss support group is, so that I will be able to help myself and others not enter similar wars anymore. That's what drives me now, more than anything: the hope that now, through my quiet introspective ways, I will be able to see reasons for positive action, for lasting through despair as it comes.

The physical world as I know it has been battered so badly recently that it might not survive despite many positive efforts, but that doesn't mean that people living on this plane, as I am, as animals and plants do, couldn't reach a higher level of awareness before the planet self-destructs, a level high enough to transcend physical destruction, to go beyond limitations of various kinds to the point of transferring one's essence to other planes, so that when regeneration does take place this essence may return and contribute vital information.

As Nonna has guided me for so many years beyond the time of her death, so the essential nature of those who live fully may be able to guide those who will plant new roots when they're needed. I will remain present, living with the little fear of the unknown as is only natural, but not with the fear of death, since I think of death as a transition, since I know myself to be functioning with awareness.

I am sustained by the essence of The Way, or what others call God, and will continue to be, through a final rite of passage when it is my turn, because I am aware that the force behind life itself can't be destroyed all at once everywhere. Plants die in some ways more quickly and in other ways more slowly than humans; some become wood that houses and furniture are made of, and yet retain their essential nature when treated with respect. Some animals become food and yet pass on their positive essence when treated with that same respect. And destruction, as wide-spread as it may be, still leaves signs of what was, to those who know how to read them, if only so that pains will be taken to keep destruction from happening again in the same way, in the future.

It is in this sense that awareness allows for transcendence, here and now, through my scribbles in this notebook, through my cat's sleeping at my feet, through the cool dreary day out, through the loud voices of my neighbors in the hallway. Elsewhere, there are people just coming out of church, or just waking to the new day, or working to put food on the table. Some are grieving for people they love, some are taking the opportunity to love their children, some are contorted with harmful needs they can't or won't control. I still have to be here, I still have to make and eat my lunch, to be kind to my plants and animals, to seek guidance and reassurance from those I will interact with today, because the more my own awareness includes others, the more I see things from multiple perspectives, which is helpful in understanding more.

I was forty-eight this year, I will be forty-nine soon, but in case there really are thirty more years ahead for me here, my job is to stay open and aware from now on. In time there will be a regular job, maybe, a spouse, maybe, a more permanent home, but for any of those to come I need to continue functioning exactly as I am, despite old 'negative core beliefs', until they change, despite disappointments, despite things that come so far out of left field that I can't prepare for them no matter what I do. I have to be here, in the moment.

Tuesday morning. I woke up with a deep feeling of unease again today. Yesterday I typed up the notes from the other day. I fed the cats, made the bed, and was going to go to the library to print out what I had, but it feels like I need to write some more, instead. I choose to think that the pain of healing is what is taking place. I am feeling polluted again, almost helpless, but I do have pen and paper, and will use them to get through the day.

It occurred to me last night that before focusing on getting a job I need to get past this dread of living, if that's what it is. I am nervous again about going where I'm invited for Thanksgiving, and then to the high school reunion. If I am so nervous about two pleasant social events, how could I hold down a job, or even get a job? Something has to shift first, my sense of inadequacy must be allowed to diminish, and later be gently held in check.

I am in crisis again, like I was as a child in Romania at the age of twelve, terrified of what's around the corner. Until that part of me heals, these bouts of inadequacy will continue. What I am sure of, beyond the counseling I'm getting and the positive influence of my current support group, is that I have to go through the process. As they say in the group, "you can't go over it, you can't go under it, you can't go around it, you have to go through it", and that's what I need to do, revisiting trauma so as to release it.

The notes I was typing up yesterday brought up my dependence on self-destructive behavior, due to not knowing any other way. Seeing the need to change that, yet feeling helpless about it, is what it's all about. I've kept thinking that if I just get to the point where things are better (the house, the job, the man), then I will finally be able to face the pain, and heal. I have lived with that assumption for thirty years, and it is only sinking in now that such a time is unlikely to come, that it can't come until I deal with my pain where I am, and as I am, right now, not later. Otherwise I would be just bringing in pollution to any positive environment. I need to face my sense of failure where I stand. Luckily, I am at a point at which, and in an environment in which, that can happen.

And I am living in an apartment that has witnessed several major events in my life, an apartment from which I've wanted to get away, seeing living here as a reflection of my failure in general. I have hoped that the new medication and the sense of acceptance as to my mental illness would finally do away with my sense of failure as a matter of fact, but that hasn't happened. My 'negative core beliefs' are still stronger than I can handle, much of the time.

I have hoped to find work which would distract me from my sense of failure. Volunteering at the drop-in center was about that, as any job would be for the same reason right now – I was trying to prove that I am worthy, as if I'm not. I have compared myself to my sister, to others, and found myself lacking. As much as I see the need to let go of so much hurt in the past, I find myself in the Catch-22 of needing to be already somewhere else, in a place I can't picture myself getting to because I feel unworthy. I return to the same stumbling block whenever I think about it, and yet I can't give up now.

It is not how others see me. Others tend to see me as positive, able, and strong, but I still see myself as bound by my family's disappointments. And yet there is no other way but to show up every day, to continue to chip away at the barrier until it falls. Part of my life has been that persistence all along. I need to honor that process by not giving up now. This morning I feel more beat-up than usual, but I need to document the feeling so I can look at it later and learn from it. Trusting in the process of recovery involves action, and standing my ground now through taking notes is part of that action.

What I sense most right now is a great impatience with not having gotten past this same barrier to functioning well, already. As if the core belief that was set in place by my family's discontentment with my bipolar disorder is being dumped on me in larger quantities. I still hear my mother's disappointment and feel it as that heavy load, as if it just won't go away. I want to accomplish something, just to be able to say – See, I'm better than that, I'm worthy of more, of love, of compassion.

I continue to dodge debilitating blows the best I can, but some still get through. But this is how it's done, moving forward, just persisting in getting myself to safety; going to work immediately, once in the safe haven, on patching up the open wounds, preparing for the next rally. I thought the battle was over, I thought the war was won, but it turns out that recovery requires action, as well as the willingness to be healed. What is obvious to me now is that the safe haven does exist in me, and in my home. The medication is working, I have created a reality of financial stability which will allow for a concerted recovery effort, and there is harmony at home, with myself and the cats.

What I was typing up last night, about my addiction to dependent behavior, about my 'negative core belief' of inadequacy, is what I'm wrestling with right here and now in my home. As if I am experiencing withdrawal, which really is the case. I have plenty of food for myself and the cats for today, so I don't need to go out to get more, and doing printing at the library can wait. But I get the feeling that I have to go, I have to get out. I get the feeling of being pushed out of my own life again, as I have many times in the past. But I will stand my ground, do this writing longhand until I'm done, and control my impulse to seek solace in anything but staying home.

I need to turn the tables on my own impulses today, and just stay put. I don't have to go anywhere, I don't have to prove anything to anyone, not even to myself. Whatever force is pushing at me will fail, finally, today. After today, possibly more weary than ever, I will go see my therapist tomorrow as scheduled, and will make it somehow to Thanksgiving dinner and the reunion on Saturday. There is no magic pill, I just have to get through the withdrawal, since that's what it is. I've been able to downplay all other factors, I don't have to be anywhere, so this will be my last stand, for today. My environment will allow for it.

Another day. It's still early; somehow I have to get through the whole day. But once again I will check the facts, as my therapist would suggest. The rent is paid, all the bills are paid, there is food and fresh water. The apartment is clean and neat. At most I need to do some vacuuming. The cats are taking their morning naps. I already ate breakfast. I don't owe anything to anyone in this life.

Which brings up an important point: part of my inadequacy for so long has been the sense of owing others. My mother drilled that into me thoroughly and I'm still having trouble with it. Luckily, that particular struggle is over. A year after my mother's death, I am grateful for what she set aside for me financially and I feel that I've used it well, disproving her expectations of my becoming homeless shortly after her death. I have not had to sell out in any way, due to her generosity. For that I am very grateful, and that helps me see her need to direct my life from a neutral point, finally.

Though I am not bound to do it in any physical way, I am willing to live through this, as yet another stage of withdrawal. It may be unpleasant, but running away from it would only mean that I have to come back to deal with it later, which I'm no longer willing to do. I got plenty of rest last night, I've eaten, I feel balanced enough to take on this challenge. Now I will refuse to vacate the premises, literally and figuratively. No one is actually pushing me out, and there is no emergency to be addressed, there are no calls to be answered. There is no storm on the horizon. So I will stay put. My knee still hurts, so I couldn't go walking or swimming anyway. There is nothing to distract me from this point of passage.

Later I will type up these notes, and get them ready to print, tomorrow I will do grocery shopping to last me through the long weekend. More white hairs will show up, as they have been. I may be able to function and no more, not excel, but that is alright. There is no more waiting until things are a little better before I head out to take care of the needs in my life. I am here now, protected by the will of God as I've prayed for it, without any armor as such, but heartened by Nonna's ability to stand with me, as she always has. That much love will be enough. I will survive the torrent of my 'negative core beliefs' today, then I will drag myself to shore and walk away. Tomorrow, and the next day, and the next, if they find me again, I will do the same thing.

What I notice, along with Dr.Low's idea *that there is only the sense of security or insecurity at any one time,* never both, is that, when I'm having insecure thoughts, the sense of failure is complete. What my therapist and I talk about often, getting grounded, is what leads me out of that state. Dr.Low called that *substituting secure thoughts for insecure thoughts.* It is doable. Even when the secure thought seems difficult to believe, it is important to be persistent in supplying it, despite physical, emotional, or mental discomfort. Taking distance from the sense of being overwhelmed is essential; even just a small distance will make a difference. That is what I am doing now, taking a little distance, while staying engaged in the process of denying the need to continue giving way to 'negative core beliefs.' No one else can do that for me, not even a future self that has already been healed. I have to stand my ground as I am, and I'm doing it.

It has been a very difficult year, but enough healing has happened already to allow for this stand now. If all I do is keep scribbling, then watch a movie, then scribble some more, then watch another movie, then type out what I've scribbled, that will be enough. There is no perfect moment other than this. The mental fatigue that hits me when I feel inadequate in my life is real, and yet I must take it blow after blow as it comes; I must retreat a little through rest, and then regroup, get through some more. The malaise I feel isn't part of the illness, it is a reaction to shifting away from ingrained behavior. That is an important distinction.

None of what I'm doing internally is likely to be noticed by others. There is, to them, just my body laid out on the couch with pen and paper in hand; but something is happening. Later I will thank my cats as well as I can for bearing with my need to focus on writing today. They have retreated to the bedroom, for the time being.

I come to acceptance, again. I knew my mother was sick, I guessed that she wouldn't last long, yet I didn't go see her. I put myself first and she died, without me there. Does that make me partly responsible? Would it have changed things if I'd agreed to have energy shifted again from my own self, according to old patterns? Here is the deeper question: was I ever able to "make it better" for my father, the one who established the pattern in the first place? The answer is yes, I made a difference, but one so small and for such a short time that a path of depletion had to be established. And then the need was amplified, as if my compassion were a drug that my father came to dependent on.

My way of leaving relationships and places has been to shift compassion originating in me to another outside recipient. What I haven't done before, but am in the process of doing now, is to no longer shift any form of energy of my own to someone else until I've healed, and then to do it only in small quantities, so as not to get drained again to the point of exhaustion. It's hard because that's all I've ever done, but it needs to happen.

Nonna helped me replenish that energy while she was still alive, and has done so at crucial times since her death; she is there for me right now. Her connection with me, my connection with her, is intact. I pray for her help, and it comes. As she is not separate from God, she brings me healing that could only come through God, as much as through her own goodwill. It is partly her hand that moves across the page, especially on a day like today. She hasn't given up on me, ever. She is part of The Way. Her love comes through. I follow her, hand in hand at times, as I did when I was a child. My self having been fragmented since that time, I need to go back to that reset point, as it were, of love without expectations, because love hasn't been the same since.

As I get healthier, it is confirmed that unconditional love is the only kind of love I am capable of, emotionally as well as physically, and that the impulse to love in that way is the only way that will ever make sense to me. I just have to learn to curb my need to rescue those who look desperate, whether they really are or not.

Nonna was able to save her love and compassion for me. I need to know that I can curb my own love and compassion. When it was time, she didn't hesitate to die, knowing that her death was only a transition, that she could still reach me whenever I needed her. That is what gives me strength. That is what reminds me of moments when I've had my feet firmly planted on the ground, on days like today, or whenever I feel I'm slipping. She has been very patient, waiting for the right opportunity to guide me out of that old destructive pattern of exhausting myself in the attempt to please others. With her by my side, I can rebuild my life. My mother wasn't able to be that person for me, and neither was my father. But I can be that person for myself. Love allows for it.

Going to the reunion last night was a little like going back to Romania for the first time. That time, it seemed like everything had shrunk because I had been a child when I left. This time it seemed strange to see how much my classmates had changed in the last thirty years. I've seen my sister change over time, but gradually, not all at once. I had been worried about not having much to show for my life so far, but it turned out to be enough that I looked young, much like they remembered me. I hadn't expected that reaction because I've lived all these years fully and I thought it would show. It was just nice to get compliment after compliment. I had a nice time.

When I came home, still struggling with excitement, it was great to have my cats there, to have them take part in it. I took my meds and had to lie still in bed with the cats by my side before the excitement would subside. I'd had a similar feeling two nights earlier, when I came back from Thanksgiving dinner at my friends'.

I had braced myself for both nights out, thinking I might have to deal with the subject of my being bipolar. That goes to show that part of me is still on guard for a question my mother used to ask: "Do they know?", as if people should be warned about my being bipolar, as if when I don't mention it right away I am being an impostor. Yet another behavior to unlearn. The sense of being "damaged goods" to the point that other people should be warned against me hasn't left me yet.

It felt alright telling the people who asked what I'm doing now that I'm in the middle of another transition, that I'm optimistic about learning some computer skills in the new year so that I can reenter the work force, after years of doing massage on my own. It came up over Thanksgiving dinner that my friend's husband is a volunteer instructor in a program with just that aim, being offered free of charge in Elizabeth. It's clearly the next step for me. So far, my computer skills have been about writing, and layouts for the massage newsletter I used to put out. This will be different. To work in an office I will need more skills than I have now.

What was as important as just showing up at the reunion was finding out that I've made it through the past thirty years doing what I needed to do to keep going. That is reassuring, looking back, because despite many periods of financial insecurity somehow I always got by, so I'm likely to, from now on also. Somehow I've maintained or acquired a certain youthfulness in the process, but more importantly I am finally functioning in a sustainable way.

What I return to this Sunday morning is that I really do have a chance to start fresh, this time with only a residue of the old familiar nagging criticisms to filter out. Over time the sum of that residue will decrease, although it is reasonable to assume that the process will be life-long. *There are no uncontrollable impulses, just those impulses we choose not to control,* but controlling them doesn't mean trying to wipe them out. Again, it turns out that sometimes behavior is as addictive as anything else, certainly as any substance.

In our most recent session my therapist mentioned that addictive behaviors have something to do with unpredictable outcomes. If we knew exactly what play to make, the thrill would go out of it. But since we don't know for sure, we take chances on the unpredictable rather than be contented with what we have. Something like my impulse the other day to get out and accomplish something rather than be contented with staying home: what I call being pushed out of my own life by a sense of inadequacy. But I did alright the last time the impulse came, I stood my ground and did some writing instead, trusting in the process.

Whether I learned impulsive behavior from my mother or on my own is no longer an issue. The more important thing is to make the effort to unlearn it, steadily, for the rest of my life, without being too distressed about minor setbacks. I don't need to perform anymore, just to keep my mother's criticism at bay. I just need to address my own 'negative core beliefs.' That is essential. From now on I can concentrate on the process of recovery.

As much as this past year it has been very strange not to have to answer to my mother anymore, it continues to be a surprise how much I've lived in hiding in general. Going out this weekend has been a big step, even more so because my choices were well thought-out rather than impulsive. I knew I would have some fearful anticipation about both, when it came to it, but I also knew it was important to show up, not to expect too much and just get through it. And I did. These two small victories now allow me to plan more things, like continuing to show up for the loss support group, tonight and through the holidays at least, and to follow through with the computer skill building program. With that sustained effort, things will continue to budge.

Part of the process for me is finding out what situations I can handle, if only in small quantities, even though other people can handle them in large quantities daily, and not to push beyond what I can handle. The drop-in center is a good example of that. I tried to force myself to stay on there as a volunteer facilitator, this past May and June, though I didn't feel comfortable doing it. When several situations that I didn't know how to handle came up, I sank into a sense of failure and couldn't recover, ending in a complete withdrawal from the center. It was much like the sense of failure I've had in the past when I felt compelled to leave massage jobs, and others before. Instead of considering whether the job was suitable for me or not in the first place, I kept taking up whatever came my way and applying all my effort to it, seeking approval. When the approval was either partial or failed to come, the 'automatic thoughts' of my not being enough to satisfy took me to the point of quitting very quickly, with the sense of failure amplified.

As much as what was being reinforced through that process was the confirmation that my mother was right in being disappointed in me in general, now that she's gone it's important to steer these damaging 'automatic thoughts' out of the main thoroughfares of my mind. They won't disappear altogether, just as I won't ever be able to erase the feeling I had when my ex-husband called me "damaged goods," but I will be able to function despite the sinking feeling regardless of the degree to which it still exists.

Another thing that I need to keep doing is to stay away from regular television other than in times of emergency. Weeks ago with the terrorist attacks in Paris I felt helpless to do anything, again, watching the aftermath on television and very quickly noticing how infectious were the unchecked commentaries of various news people. I withdrew almost right away, finding it to be too much for me. Once again, what was happening seemed like sensationalism on top of very serious circumstances. I don't know why the distinction isn't as important to others as it is to me, but as long as I can't find a news station that does see the importance of it, I will have to refrain from following current events closely.

Considering my losses again through the grief seminar, I noticed that I listed rape at the age of twenty-two, but didn't mention my first psychiatric hospitalization as part of it. We had been asked to make a list of our losses. Also, I didn't mention my other hospitalizations. I didn't purposely exclude them either, but it seems evident to me now that I never allowed myself to grieve for that collective loss. It was more important to get past it, to bury it. Maybe I should consider the sense of loss related to those hospitalizations now.

The first was the most striking, due also to my family's reaction to it in general, as well as due to the rape. What happened afterward was more about that reaction than about trying to get well. Whatever I had accomplished in my college years had been instantly nullified. I have mentioned the circumstances in my writing before, but always with the feeling that I could never retrieve my reputation after the fact. Going to the high school reunion gave me a boost because a whole set of people had a positive reaction to me. One person had just recovered from cancer and felt very at ease talking about it. I hope in time I will be as comfortable talking about the circumstances of my initial breakdown. It's an odd thing, on thinking of it again now: my parents knew, when I was diagnosed, that what I had was a chemical imbalance, which, as doctors, they knew could be addressed with medication. There was no need to see me as a lost cause. But their shame regarding me was so strong that it became the deciding factor in their attitude.

School had just ended. I didn't have the support structure I'd had up to that point because everyone moved on after graduation. But Stephan came to stay with me at my parents' for two weeks. We'd met at a party in New York that winter. I was supposed to go visit him in Germany but didn't make it. I clung to him for approval, after my hospitalization, and for hope. My parents allowed me to go spend some time with him in Italy later that summer. He told me he thought I wasn't bipolar. I didn't tell him I'd been raped in the hospital because I believed it when the hospital staff told me that if I told him he wouldn't want me anymore. I had already become damaged goods in my mind, though I wouldn't hear the expression until many years later.

I wanted to start fresh with Stephan; not being bipolar would be part of it. So the following year, in 1990, when we lived together in Italy for six months, I stopped taking my lithium. I got angry with him when he said "Well, I probably have to marry you now", and I returned to New York without plans of seeing him again. I can see now that my anger then was due to mood swings, but I couldn't then. I was scheduled to have a show in New York that summer so I was due back anyway; I had worked hard on a series of new paintings in Italy to complement the ones I already had. I was counting on success. I didn't know that, at least for me, part of mania is pushing away anything that passes for failure. It gets buried without going away, and then eventually it has to be dug up and considered before one can move on. But at the time all I did was not acknowledge it. Failure was too painful to look at. I was denying my past much as my parents had, in coming to the U.S.

I didn't see my actions as part of a pattern, though they were: at the slightest obstacle to a smooth flow of events my anger rose to the point that I had to deny the particular course of action I was on. Asking for help wasn't an option. I had to set things right on my own, by myself, but by that point I didn't have the patience to do it. To make up for my previous failures, I had to come up with a sweeping success that would do away with the sense of loss. I never had a plan B. I never considered my overall health.

In the meantime, I became more and more financially dependent on my parents. They paid for Italy, they paid for the show, they helped me with the rent in Brooklyn where I was living while I was taking acting classes in the fall of '90. I took odd job after odd job but couldn't pay the bills. I think my father was hoping for a blinding success for me as much as I was, something that would set it all right. My mother went along with it, but without any faith.

I believe now what they told me later, that they helped me because they were afraid of me, and for me. I got my way, I got my show, but nothing sold and my plans for success died away. My depression grew when I got pregnant by a classmate in acting school, who was as young and broke as I was. My parents said they would support me through the pregnancy and afterward only if I moved in with them and committed to staying in Cranford for good. I had an abortion instead, but moved back to Cranford because I was too depressed to work.

When I did start coming out of my depression I decided to try to escape again. My old roommate had suggested working on an NYU student film production to get me out of the funk I was in, and it worked. When that production was over there was another little one, and then I asked my parents to let me go to Romania for the summer. I spent ten weeks in Bucharest, staying with my uncle, spending much time just walking around. It was an interesting time to be there because the political shift at the time was still very new, and people were excited and enthusiastic.

I met Peter Brook at a press conference there, and as a direct result of that I met Florentina. She recognized me at the post office as the person who got up to do a simple acting exercise with him. Florentina and I became friends, being of the same age, and she took me around. I wanted her to come to the U.S. My uncle in the meantime had followed through on my request to find a house with a garden for me to buy. There was one on sale for five thousand dollars, on the outskirts of town. My mother said she would bring the money in person. I wanted to set up a home base for myself there.

My mother did come, but not with the intention of buying the house for me. She came to take me back to the States, where we clashed again and I was hospitalized, again. Later that summer I had such a powerful reaction to an injection of Haldol, that afterwards it was all I could do to crawl around my parents' house for months. I applied for disability from the state and was granted a monthly stipend in the spring of '92. As soon as it came through, I planned my escape again.

This time I took a bus out to Montana, where a friend I'd had at the Cooper Union had returned after graduation. We had been close, and she invited me to come and stay with her for awhile. I had no plans to return to New Jersey, but when my mother was hospitalized after having a stroke I did go back, and stayed for a month while she had open-heart surgery and recovered. I returned to Montana when my sister came from Switzerland to spend some time. She had moved there in '89.

Somehow I heard about a graduate painting program in Amsterdam and applied. They wanted to see me and my work in person, so I went, but didn't get in. Meanwhile my parents paid my travel expenses, and they vouched for Florentina so she could come visit me that summer. I returned to the States from Amsterdam the same day Florentina was due to come, and we got on the next bus to Montana together. There was someone she wanted to go see in Seattle, someone she'd kept in touch with after he'd seen her in a theater production in Bucharest.

When we got back to Missoula, fate took a hand. We met Florentina's future husband and my future husband, both named David, within a day of each other. Florentina and her husband are still together, living in San Francisco. That winter of '92 I moved up to be with my David, in Canada. I had finally escaped my family. We got married a year later. Florentina and her David came, so did my parents, who were relieved that I had succeeded in finding a husband. So did my newly divorced sister with her new boyfriend.

Thus my financial life rambled, always with help from my parents, always tied directly to the need to come up with a major success. All the time I was trying to deny I was bipolar. I stopped taking my lithium the year leading up to my marriage. My parents didn't approve, when I finally told them, but I was planning to show them different. Instead, I needed to be hospitalized again in the spring of '94, and into the summer. This time I told myself it was my husband's fault, as well as my parents'. I had gone to a spiritual seminar that my husband had insisted I go to, and it had torn me apart, leading to an extended manic episode. Afterward, neither my parents nor my husband wanted me. David did change his mind eventually, when I'd become stable again, and I stayed.

Only then did I start taking medication regularly. And, that summer, I started writing. I put together my life up to that point in a manuscript and sent it off to ten publishing houses in the States, all of which turned it down. But this time the sense of failure wasn't overwhelming. Eventually, in '95 or '96, David's cousin Lillian introduced me to PRH in Edmonton, through which I started therapy in earnest. PRH used writing as a tool, in group settings. I found it to be very effective.

In the fall of '96 I left my husband but chose to stay in Alberta. I was involved with someone for a few months, then we broke up and I moved into a neighboring summer village where I set up a photography and portrait studio, again with help from my parents. I put the divorce through myself, without asking for compensation. I had started to earn some money of my own in '97, when my cousin suggested that I give the art world one more chance, this time with the landscape photography I'd been doing. She set up a show for me with the Romanian embassy in Washington, DC through her contacts there, then she set up a meeting for me with the cultural attache at the Romanian consulate in New York. I went for it. We settled on a month-long show at the consulate gallery in the summer of '98. It was my parents again who paid for my trips, for the framing of the artwork, for the catalogs that were printed. I chose to detach from reality again, hoping for the one success that would make it all alright.

The people who came to see my work liked it, but nothing sold; no future shows were planned. Then I clashed with my mother again, and she had me taken to the hospital again. Because of that hospitalization I had to leave Canada for good. My Minister's Permit had been issued in '94 on condition that I would eventually support myself, and that there would be no further hospitalizations. So I returned to Brooklyn in September of '98, having given up my life, my dog, and the sense of emotional stability I'd worked so hard to get.

I got a job but was so depressed that I had trouble keeping it; I was hospitalized that first winter, then I got another job that was better and started going to therapy, but I couldn't afford therapy on my own and made the mistake of asking my mother to pay for it. That refreshed my sense of dependence.

My mother and I clashed regularly, and by the fall of '99 she refused to continue paying for my therapy. I entered a psychotic state when that happened, and eventually ended up in the hospital again in December and almost died of kidney failure. My body was strong enough to recover, however, and in the year 2000 I finally went to work on recovery on several levels: I took my medication as prescribed, I got therapy, and I applied for government help, and got it, in the way of housing, massage school, and a monthly stipend.

Meanwhile my father's Alzheimer's was progressing. I took on the role of caregiver to both my parents, since my mother's hips were worn out and she had difficulty walking. Later she was diagnosed with macular degeneration, which leads to blindness, so I felt better doing as much of the driving as possible for both of them.

In the fall of '04 my father contracted the West Nile virus and almost died. Though he recovered, his mental illness had intensified, and I stopped doing massage work so as to be available to help my mother with him full-time. That put me in a financially dependent position again until after my father's death in 2007. It was almost a year before I returned to work doing massage, at that point.

My mother moved back to Romania to live five years ago, in 2010. I had insisted on having her driving privileges taken away as her sight grew worse, and she never forgave me for it. I left the relationship I was in by getting into a brief relationship with another man. I moved into the apartment I live in now, and continued working, passed my national massage exam again that fall, did my best to prove to myself and to my mother that I was finally self-sufficient. Throughout, during the conversations we had on the phone, she would remind me of how ill she thought I was.

In the summer of 2011 I went to see my mother in Romania for the last time, to prove to her that I was alright. I kept writing, and kept publishing; I had gone to work in earnest on publishing my own writing starting in 2008. It gave me great satisfaction to document my recovery as I saw it, but I had stopped getting therapy in '07 and stopped seeing my psychiatrist in the fall of 2011.

My debt and my spending increased again, and I was unable to hold on to massage work, other than with my own clientele. Criticism had become hard to handle again. I was taking a homeopathic version of lithium and thought I could cope with things that way. I was, but only partially, and only until the summer of 2014, when both my mother and my father-figure in Cranford, Mr.Greulich, were diagnosed with cancer. As time passed, there was pressure to have me go see my mother one more time, but I didn't, and I withdrew more instead, the first week of November 2014, when they both died.

Eventually I entered a psychotic state one early morning in January, and was taken to the hospital. The result of that hospitalization is my current progressive recovery: effective medication, group and individual counseling, balanced nutrition and sleep, and a gradual effort to see myself as belonging in my own life. I have been living on savings alone since I injured my right knee badly enough in September to have to consider other work, which brings me to the need for more computer skills so I can get a regular job. In the end, my mother didn't have me taken out of her will, as I feared she would. That gives me time to get myself on my feet.

I had to hold on to myself to get this far, and I did. What will come next is an integration of all my skills and abilities. My aim is balance, and I believe it will come. The medication and therapy have brought me this far in a relatively short time, and there is plenty of hope for me as I find myself more and more able to function in the world around me, as I did this weekend.

I will be forty-nine in two months, and I take heart in knowing that my father was able to start his life over at fifty, on coming to the U.S. There's hope for me too. There were no guarantees then, and there are none now, but there is hope, and faith. I will have to continue to develop that faith in myself for it to work; much of that has to do with addressing 'negative core beliefs', as I am doing. I don't need to take on challenges that are too great for me. Dealing with what there is, daily, is enough. The point will be not to try to obliterate 'negative core beliefs', but to allow them to die down to the point of becoming a mild irritation and no more. I think I can do that, with the help I'm getting.

I used to think damage that great could only be addressed while in a supportive relationship with a life partner, but since there isn't one I need to do it on my own, and am finding that it is possible. I have the unconditional love of my two cats. That goes a long way on a daily basis. Also, my apartment feels harmonious, which makes a difference. I used to think that I needed to own my own home before I could feel this much at ease. It's the concerted effort to accept my own life that makes more of a difference. With that in place, I was able to show up at my high school reunion without "the house", "the job" or "the guy", and I'm able to continue showing up to my loss support group until I've fully grieved my mother's death. I'm doing the work, and it counts.

What has been consistent for so many years is that writing is my most effective tool in reaching a balanced state. I had put it aside with the therapy and the medication, but now it's back, and it's allowing me to function, to rebuild faith and hope in myself. For that I'm grateful. With discipline, it will be able to lead me out of a depressed state on a regular basis, with increasing potency. It's no longer about proving anything; it's about reflecting what is, with enough distance so it can do me good. That is enough.

Sunday morning. Maybe some of the anxiety I'm feeling is related to a cleanse I'm doing, or maybe I'm just getting in the way of my 'automatic thoughts' again. I've been 'daring to exist', as they used to say in PRH, by going ahead with plans to publish more of my writing. The Christmas tree looks good, with popcorn garlands and all-red ornaments. The Kiddo likes to play with some of them, Vinny likes to chase her around.

I'm helpless again with the feeling that my mother can still do me harm. I wonder if psychotic elements used to overlap with 'automatic thoughts', for me. Could my mother still cause me harm? Was she ever able to? Am I defying her again by standing up for myself, by going ahead now with my writing? Will my defiance mean that there will be hell to pay?

I will insist on going to the loss support group tonight. I found myself feeling responsible, lately, for someone's recent illness in the group. I went as far as to ask myself if she's getting punished as a lesson to me for daring to ask for help. My meds are on track, so I know I'm not psychotic. The only other explanation is an overlap, in the past, of paranoia and the sense of not being enough, of being unable to protect those I care about. I still fear that when I say No to abuse, damage will come to others.

I notice that I've been thinking about The Little One again this week, with the recurring idea that I should have been able to cure her hyperactive thyroid through sheer will. When I got her two years ago it was with the general idea that, in my home, the hyperactivity would taper off. Helplessness related to such feelings is debilitating, but *helplessness is not hopelessness*. I keep worrying that when I think of the people responsible for positive change in my life, I open them up to having something bad happen to them. I felt that about my dog Blue and my old cat Josie, about my grandmother, about other people. As if standing up for me or with me puts people in jeopardy, even retroactively, opening them up to a direct line of fire of trigger-happy enemies, known or unknown.

I tell myself there's no logic in it, but where I get confused is when I remember times that I've been right about things that happened, like dreaming about my ex-husband's involvement with another woman while he was away at a seminar shortly after we got married. I was also very aware that something was wrong with Blue the day he was in a severe accident. My ex-husband, under whose care I had left him to go have my show in New York in '98, insisted that there was nothing wrong with him. He'd wanted to spare me coming home early, he told me later. But if I'd returned early, my mother wouldn't have hospitalized me at the end of the show and I might not have had to leave Canada for good. I have learned to trust my gut more since then. Though I also know, again through Recovery, that *we know that we don't know*. Something even harder to bear might have happened if I'd returned early.

The night of the Paris terrorist attacks a month ago I was watching Déjà Vu, with Denzel Washington. I found out about the situation in Paris on the radio, on my way to Barnes&Noble. I'd found the storyline of the movie, which was about a terrorist attack, disturbing enough that I wanted a break from it. Instead, when I heard about the attacks, at least initially, I felt that my anxiety had spilled into real life. I got myself another movie but I also got Benjamin Hoff's TAO OF POOH and TE OF PIGLET, which I'd read before, to get me through it. They kept me grounded while the news coverage subsided. I was right in anticipating that I'd be drawn to the TV and at the same time feel overwhelmed by events I could do nothing about. Writing helped then too, as it does now.

I still feel it though, even as I apply logic. I feel guilt related to any incident I hear about, as if someone else is being punished instead of me when I remove myself from the line of fire. I feel a sense of responsibility as I pay attention to events around me. I want to say "take me, instead of my people." In the light of day, with a little distance, it seems absurd to feel this way, but when the waves of automatic thoughts hit, it becomes real. Then, I want to say "Take me on, mother, instead of them," like I used to say to myself when my mother was still alive. She had told my boyfriend once that she could put a curse on him if she wanted to, because she was a witch and she had done it before. I believed her, though maybe I shouldn't have. It's been a problem, not knowing what to believe but feeling that my thoughts or actions could make a difference.

P_{art} T_{hree}

Home just after the loss support group, I have to get this down. Something about my anxiety in general never clicked quite this way before: lately, and for the past year, the anxiety I've felt has been that of my twelve-year-old self. I've been revisiting the feeling and the memory of the events leading up to leaving Romania that first time, and things have been coming up vividly. I had a very high level of anxiety then, which was never dealt with.

It was important that the counselor tonight pointed out something that I'd heard before - that anxiety is always about the future. Since I always thought of that first anxious time as a major cause of depression, I forgot that anxiety is about the future. This weekend, thinking about meeting up with my new job coach was about anxiety. Worrying about parking in Elizabeth while I take my computer-skill-building course starting in January is about anxiety. But worrying about the effect of past behavior is not the same. That falls under depression. It was good to have that distinction made. Also, something simple but difficult was addressed – that for beliefs to change, new behavior must be practiced, even if it's uncomfortable.

Every time I feel anxiety again, I will remind myself that such times are opportunities to stop and address my twelve-year-old self's sense of terror. My sense of security had been turned upside down, and it was never set back to a neutral position. It started with my uncle's filling me in, through intense sessions, on the political history of our family and of Romania in general. What I had known as safe and normal was abruptly filled in as threatening. My uncle's intention was, no doubt, to reassure me that my parents had made the right decision in defecting, but that intention missed its mark and created a silent terror in me instead. What I was learning turned out to be that I couldn't depend on anything being what I thought it was.

Then, coming to the U.S., and having trouble fitting in, confirmed the feeling of dread. After that, all efforts were made to concentrate on future success, always pushing forward with that aim. When my world collapsed, with the original diagnosis of manic depression, all hopes of a normal productive life were lost. I had striven for perfection and was abruptly faced with the certainty that I would never attain it. The underlying goal, of pleasing my parents through success, was nullified. From the time of my first hospitalization on, the goal was modified to making them less ashamed of me, if I could. I didn't realize then, nor for these past twenty-six years, that the effort was unnatural. It just was what I did, it was all I knew.

With my mother's death, the boulder I was pushing uphill fell by the wayside, never to be recovered. I lost even that bent purpose. That led to anxiety as intense as on leaving Romania that first time, much compounded by the fear that with both my parents gone I was slated for financial ruin. It was as if all the skills I've gathered along the way these past thirty-six years had evaporated.

Now, with having to give up massage for a living too, due to my knee injury, that dread has intensified. Impending doom is my reality, when I can't distract myself from it. My collapse last winter was as much about the intense isolation due to extreme anxiety, as about the chemical imbalance due to the disruption of my medication. Getting back on track with the meds has allowed me to start benefitting from therapy again, and has helped me maintain an even keel as far as anxiety is concerned. However, as I confront the belief that all I can be as a person with bipolar disorder is a failure, as I insist on moving past this belief to a more productive outlook, anxiety continues to surface.

I am anxious about waking up on time to go meet my job coach tomorrow, I am anxious about getting kicked out of Barnes&Noble for sitting in their coffee shop for too long, even before either has happened. I am kicking myself for having suggested it so that we could meet as early as nine o'clock because that's what the job coach wanted. The fear of embarrassment is intense, as intense as it was surrounding Thanksgiving and my high school reunion. It was extreme also as to the process of submitting the necessary information regarding the new book. Now that it's done, I have moved on to having anxiety about what the editorial staff will think when they read it. I live in a heightened state of anxiety to which there seems to be no end.

And yet, I show up in my life, and I do things I set out to do, daily. Sometimes I'm even capable of spontaneous action. By just showing up, no matter how challenged I feel, I am practicing changing my behavior, a little like with exams in college. There is the feeling that there will be only small breaks in the tension. But college exams were supposed to lead to a college diploma, and they did. What was so difficult about that was that an accomplishment that great coincided with the great disillusionment of finding out I could never redeem myself in my parents' eyes.

Being diagnosed with bipolar disorder meant that I had become a failure, and it had happened overnight. It was an unsurmountable disappointment. I kept trying, one way or another, to get past it, to get around it, but it never worked, for a simple reason: I never took the time to heal. All my efforts were about patching myself up so I could keep going, keep trying to amount to something.

My job coach isn't daunted. His job is to help me find work and he's willing to go headlong into it, without hesitation. I, meanwhile, am still anticipating collapse even after the job is landed. The obstacles to getting a job are almost comforting, in that they will take time and effort to overcome. I want it to be obvious that I am willing to make the effort, but following through is still unimaginable. With that thought formed, consoling thoughts come teeming in, as consoling words used to come from my mother, but only in psych emergency rooms, while I would wait to be admitted. I need to see past this coddling state to a time of more functionality. For now, anxiety and depression come in equal measure. The 'core belief' of failure is still strong.

It helps to know now, that anxiety and depression can be due to 'core beliefs', that they have influenced my reactions, but that reactions can change. That gives me hope. I have been strong before, in dealing with challenges; I was good at dealing with challenges throughout both art school and massage school. Maybe now I'll find enough strength to start over again without disproportionate expectations, without still putting myself down. Now that I'm not hearing anymore how sad it is that I've stopped painting, maybe I can start working at an entry-level job without beating myself up about it.

I never understood until now that it's not my illness that makes me insecure and anxious, but my 'automatic thinking' alongside 'negative core beliefs.' It's alright now to accept help and compassion as I make my own efforts. As a former client told me more than a year ago, Romanians are genetically predisposed to endure. I take heart in my own prolonged ability to endure until positive change can take place. That time is now. My mother isn't there anymore to help me only when I'm down. There are now people willing to show compassion as I pick myself up and move on.

It is morning, after breakfast. The job coach texted me a little while ago that he can't make it and will call to reschedule. I had already taken a shower and picked out my clothes for the day so I put them on and took the time to make a fried egg sandwich rather than just have yogurt. Last night was a good night of rest. I woke up an hour before the alarm and thought about what had come up yesterday. I revisited the time of that shift that was so disturbing in my life thirty-six years ago, this time with understanding, rather than dread or loss. Half-awake for that hour, I looked at it again.

The feeling of not being enough started there. I had thought, before my parents left, that I was real pals with my father, because he had always encouraged me to think so. That summer and fall however, with so many changes of attitude to witness, I began to doubt that it had been true at all. We, my sister and I, hadn't been told that my parents were planning to defect. It was explained to us that it was because my sister or I might have slipped and talked about it in school before it was certain that my parents could defect. There was a possibility that they couldn't, and then they would have to return, as if from vacation. If anyone would have gotten wind of their true intentions before then, they would have gone to jail.

That was the logical explanation, but my trust in my father still suffered as a result. I had always thought that we shared all important secrets. In the new light, it became clear that the traffic went only one way. With the shift, I realized that I was just a child who couldn't be trusted when push came to shove, to my father. We weren't pals after all, he was the adult and I was the child, and it was the adult, not the twelve-year-old, who made all the decisions affecting both.

But there was more to it, something that allowed for anger to build in the years to come, because it remained unaddressed: the idea that life was by definition better in the U.S. than in Romania. My sister and I were supposed to embrace that idea immediately, leaving the life we had known behind without hesitation. That was the first real problem. The sense of abandonment was there too, and it was difficult to bear for a long time that my parents gambled on being able to get us out without any logical certainty. The loss of our old life was not as obvious.

When I heard about how little we'd had as children or would have to look forward to as Romanian adults, I couldn't argue with it, but there was something about it that bothered me: my life hadn't felt lacking in any way until my parents' defection, and afterward it never felt whole. I couldn't put my finger on why. The way the standard of living deteriorated in Romania on all levels after we left showed that it was lucky we'd gotten out when we did, but there was still something about it.

That entire summer and fall I'd heard about how my life would change for the better, but having to leave my Nonna behind was so traumatic that even when she came to live with us six months later, the damage couldn't be undone. I'd thought I was losing her for good, and it was very painful to lose what had embodied wholeness for me. I had hoped that my father would have taken the opportunity to explain, immediately upon our arrival, how it had been possible to leave us behind, but he didn't. Instead he was tired, stressed and defensive, dealing with huge amounts of anxiety of his own.

What I had known in Romania, a comfortable home and a life with peers, as well as the deep sense of belonging in Nonna's life and home as an extension of my life with my parents, had been dismissed as something to be discarded. Only future material gains were to be the focus. I went from being a whole kid to being an outsider in my new environment in a very short time, and, in my sullen behavior, became a disappointment to my parents as well. They knew only to insist on my disciplining myself through school work as a way to have me snap out of it. Only I didn't snap out of it. I just became more and more frustrated. The "too sensitive" label was applied, and the general idea was to toughen me up a little, now that I knew what the real world was like.

But here comes the basis of what was the greatest challenge for me: the world that I had known in Romania *was* real, and in many ways more satisfying than the new life. I had been sheltered from adversity and then plunged directly into my parents' anxiety and exhaustion from one day to the next. Their life would be day-to-day hardship for many years. The change was so drastic, and the lack of transition so glaring, that it was impossible to function well, and yet that was just what was expected of me. I had entered directly into the maze so many American kids find themselves in, of competing for the best possible future. Since not everyone can have a satisfying life, or so I was told, looking at things realistically, since the good spots have to be fought for and then defended, growing up was more like wiping out the competition than maturing at a natural rate, whatever that might be for me.

And here it is again: as a child in Romania I knew my life as valid, only to find out that the standards by which it counted as valid could dissolve overnight. So what assurance was there that the standards I lived by in my new life wouldn't also dissolve? What went on for years was what I'd known: following the path set by my elders so as to gain their approval. Their approval mattered, because as elders they knew better. But what I didn't know, since Nonna had never disappointed in this respect, was that not all adults were elders, even if they happened to be my parents.

Nonna had granted me a sense of security, both in Romania and the U.S. In Romania she had been the family elder, but in the U.S. her status changed to a sweet old lady who let Jehova's Witnesses in when the rest of us were out living our busy lives. No one took her to church, so she allowed church to come to her, overlooking the exact denomination. She was there every morning to have coffee with my mother and speed her on her way to work, she was there to dance with me to our favorite song whenever we needed to reconnect. I was closer to her than to either of my parents.

When Nonna died it was implied that I would treat my parents as the elder she had been, that I would apply myself to satisfying their demands of me. And I did, at least for awhile, but with a twist: I began to challenge them, first by applying only to art schools when I'd only had a liberal arts training, then, when I was accepted to the Cooper Union, by refusing a safety net of practical skills. I was going to dive headlong into art without a parachute. But I went about it in a way I thought would make my parents proud: I didn't drink, I didn't smoke, I just worked really hard, even the semester when I went over to Paris.

And then something happened. While I was studying in Paris I took the opportunity to go back to Romania by train at Easter. What I saw there left me with feelings of helplessness; when I returned to New York for my senior year I wasn't sure I could go through more schooling, reality being so bleak elsewhere. I didn't have Nonna to guide me anymore. She had shown me only support, not expectations. Then my parents panicked when a friend offered me a job so that I could get grounded instead of forging ahead with more art school.

Both my parents had been kicked out of university for political reasons, and it had been difficult for them to finish their schooling afterward. They didn't want that for me, they told me. So they offered to carry my full financial load for senior year instead, as they had up to that point. It was an offer I wasn't supposed to refuse, and I didn't.

But my mental development took on a new pace, as if the world was ending and I had to get as much learning in as I could. Any sense of balance was thrown out the window. My parents didn't realize what was going on, they just insisted as they had all along that I check in with them every weekend. Our differences became more and more blatant. Then I told them, in the spring, that what I wanted was to keep on painting, so they would have to put up with paying my way some more. I was already manic, intolerant and torn up about being misunderstood. I didn't realize what was going on either. Then I crashed, but not before completing all my classes so I could graduate.

Nonna had just wanted me to be happy. My parents had needed me to be happy in the way they had hoped to be happy themselves but weren't, through accomplishment. It was alright for me to do anything I wanted with my life, as long as I was a success at it. Over time, after high school, my anger at such expectations grew, but I still didn't know enough to disengage. So I crashed.

My mother was right, I had become intolerant while still being "too sensitive" for the world around me. I think now that I just wanted to be let off the merry-go-round, to be let out of the maze of expectations I found myself in, of hopes and dreams my parents had had without being able to realize them. Since I didn't turn to drugs or alcohol, and only slightly to sex, as a release, I had nowhere to go but into the abstract aspects of art and writing, poetry and painting. Before long I lost touch with reality.

With my initial breakdown, twenty-six years ago, I crashed and burned so badly that regular work seemed out of the question. Reestablishing security seemed out of the question too. I had to get to work on redeeming myself in the eyes of my family – another goal that I didn't see as empty, though it was. I was still angry, and bent on proving them wrong about seeing me as a failure. I challenged them in all the ways that I could. Finding some sort of success would validate me again as a human being, I thought. But I kept losing my grip as I went.

What makes sense about it now is that the experience of loss really did go as far back as leaving Romania. There was something about it that I couldn't reconcile, and returning for the first time in the spring of '88 recalled for me so many unresolved feelings. I had wanted to deal with them before that, but didn't know how, so I just got on a train and went, the first chance I got. And when I got there what I saw was so nerve-wracking that I was completely at a loss to make it fit with what I'd been lucky enough to experience in my own life, growing up. I wanted to help, but I didn't know how.

One of Nonna's strengths had been her connection with God. Without her, I doubted my own. I had tried to find purpose in going to art school, and instead had found only more questions. I lost faith in myself, and the whole thing fell apart. My trust in anyone but Nonna had diminished after coming to the U.S., and what is clear to me now is that if she hadn't been there for all the time that she was, I wouldn't have stood a chance at all to recover. All I seemed to encounter were more expectations.

What had added to my confusion as to how much respect I should have for my parents was that throughout high school my father had shown interest in my physical coming of age, and my mother had showed signs of jealousy rather than an inclination to protect me. She'd told me and my sister early on that she'd stopped loving my father before we were born, but had stayed with him because he was a good father. They struggled with power over each other. My sister had the common sense to remove herself from the equation as soon as possible by having boyfriends, then by going away to college, then by leaving for good to go live in Switzerland. I stayed relatively close, still trying to get that acceptance that would never come; I became more and more dependent at every turn.

Both my parents were embarrassed and disappointed with my diagnosis of manic depression, as if it applied to them instead of me. Or as if I were an extension of them, one that just couldn't be denied, as if my failure were their own. As if mental illness in itself were a failure they hadn't counted on having to face again, having had breakdowns of their own in their early twenties, and having risen above them. What I brought them unwittingly was a reminder of the loss each of them had experienced.

I brought them shame, which was to be borne as a burden. There was no question of having a full life with a mental illness, for me. They only hoped I could deceive an unsuspecting man long enough for him to pick up the burden, but it didn't work out that way. I didn't stay married, and I didn't allow anyone close until after my father's death. So my mother and I limped along in our *temperamental deadlock*. Our pattern began in my last year in high school and ended only with my mother's death.

At this point in my life I can see that I need to *excuse and not accuse* all involved, including myself, for this behavior. I've come to know more about my father's struggle with anxiety and my mother's struggle with depression over the years. They couldn't tolerate my failure, I couldn't tolerate the sham of being expected to believe, accept and uphold that they were better than me despite having faults of their own. Financial success was always the measuring stick, and in that respect I was a failure.

So it's come full circle for me: if, after finally having financial success, my parents failed as parents in other essential ways, what was the point of leaving an old life for a new one? That brings me to where I am now. With a year's passing after my mother's death, I can now see myself asking for help: help with changing my behavior; help with coping with loss;

help with finding work and with finding the potential to be satisfied with what is, as opposed to keeping on with the inflated dreams of what should be.

I deal every day with intense anxiety, as if I wasn't supposed to move beyond losing my parents. But the fact that I did, provides me with the necessity to find a way to function. That is what brought me into a state of psychosis nearly a year ago, which prompted the hospitalization. It wasn't just relying on a homeopathic mood stabilizer instead of taking lithium that brought me into crisis. The sense of inadequacy in my own life was just too great, as well. I couldn't take it anymore, that I was supposed to put others' lives before my own. So I crashed, as if only crashing could allow for a fresh start.

My first breakdown was much the same. I couldn't make sense of my world anymore at the time, and I crashed. Every subsequent crash has had elements of the same. I sensed myself going out of control, so I crashed early so that I could be rescued. My nervous system failed to reboot on its own, time and again, until I got the help I needed, this last time too. First through medication, then through medication and therapy. Every time I felt threatened in any way, I removed myself from settings that looked alright to others but not to me. Afterward, in my isolation, I doubted my actions and fell back into cycles of anxiety and depression. These cycles became ingrained behavior. By the time of my mother's death, I had become entirely dependent on that pattern. It wasn't healthy, but it was functional. It was all that kept me going.

Massage, so positive in the work itself, was nonetheless an extension of that pattern. I was proving through massage that I had some human worth after all, through service. Now I find myself at a new beginning. I am a smart, educated, experienced twelve-year-old who never grew up. I had always been that, but now the curtain has been drawn back, like in The Wizard of Oz, and instead of an old magician there am I, paralyzed with the knowledge of being found out. Somehow I've held on to my life, but I don't know how it happened. I know that I've paid close attention whenever I've been able to, to everything that has come my way and that has allowed me to get this far, but I still need to get out of that booth, out of the driver's seat, I still need to let a grown-up lead me to a safe haven, because I simply don't have the knowledge it takes to do that. It turns out that a good part of the time it has been God, and The Way, that guided me. There is no other explanation. I wouldn't have survived without that sort of intervention. Now I need a human component as well.

This past year has been about surveying the damage done, gathering tools by the side of the road with which to begin to rebuild my ride home. But I still need a mechanic who knows how to use those tools, because there isn't a manual to go by anymore and there isn't any way for me to reinvent the wheel. My mind, if it had ever been able to synthesize information, is still so strained with past effort that I can't conceive of what amounts to the healing work that will set me straight, on my own. I need help, and since the fall what I've done is to stand up off the side of the road where people can see me so I can get a ride to the nearest town.

In my daydream, I can tell I am somewhere out west because there is the wide open road in either direction, and it doesn't matter much which way I head. I have to trust that I'm not putting myself in harm's way by making myself known. There are no indications as to what the next town might be. But the road is paved and in good repair; I have said goodbye for now to my wrecked vehicle, my life as I knew it, but I plan to come back for it when I can.

And then, from the daydream, I return to the couch I am lying on, facing my Christmas tree with the popcorn garlands and the unbreakable red decorations. My pen ran out pages ago; I am now writing in pencil in my composition notebook which I got at a bargain price at the supermarket the other day. Next time I'm out I'll buy another pen.

How did I survive this last crash and burn, and all the others? The only thing that makes sense is that there is a purpose to my life after all. I have learned what it's like to lose my way and to feel there's no going back. I can't go back to Romania. Cranford is my hometown now, and I can't quite afford it, so I live on its edge in Roselle Park, but I haven't lost my grip altogether this time. I've had to crash only a little, like with my car last year that had a bad couple of scratches, one from an accident I caused, but remained functional. I've had to crawl only a little, this time, compared to other times, and I have enough money for a roof over my head while I get my bearings. Even with all the distractions that present themselves, I will be able to pray for guidance now, and to welcome Nonna into my home again, to start the new year with her kind of faith. It has been a good morning.

Today is the thirty-sixth anniversary of my coming to the United States. I'm afraid of the future again, like I was then. My sister and I were joining our parents, after nine months of waiting to see if we'd be allowed to come. Today I feel I have nowhere to turn. I want to stay composed, but tears come anyway.

I am able to function as I need to, going to the library to meet with my job coach, getting gas, shopping for more honey and brown rice and tea. This current setback has come on strong, with insecurities to the point of not being able to distract myself even with movies. I have to hope that I can step back enough from it to be able to look at it, through my notes. I don't want to keep thinking that I can only escape anxiety now and then by pretending to be well, instead of actually being well. It can take a week for the feeling to go.

Something important came up as I was straightening up after the cats just now, first thing in the morning. I noticed that it makes me happy to see my cats happy, just as it used to be fulfilling to see other people I've cared about be happy around me. It also came up that, on my own, I only feel that happy after a day of writing, or a good walk, or a good swim. Without those, insecurities rise and self-defeatism takes hold.

Seeing my cats happy about something I've done is enough for me to want to go to the drawer I keep pen and paper in, and write, to record this little sense of happiness. Later I will be happy again, reading what I've written, and so on. In other words, doing physical tasks that please me and others allows for moments of contentment that can be renewed over time. That way a meal tastes better cooked at home, with full intent to nourish; things gain value, or value is restored.

When the reverse happens, of unexpected disrespect or lack of appreciation, the damage done can upset days or even weeks of progress, as if having to start from the bottom again. Some events may be intentional, some aren't, but it is important to *remove myself from temper-producing situations* by staying out of the way of people who might bring me harm, once they've been identified as such. Still, fear and insecurities can infiltrate without warning, despite Recovery training, despite counseling and good medication, despite the good company of my cats.

It is as if a wall rises directly in front of me, or even as if I am suddenly boxed in and have to stay that way until I figure out how to climb out of the situation, or get past it. In such moments it's as if I have to stop and recall my assets, intellectual or otherwise, as if I have to reassemble them all on the fly into whatever pattern allows for release.

What's been so disconcerting in the past is the feeling that so much of what is troublesome should have been handled by now, instead of requiring renewed effort each time. I have *temper at the illness* when I think I should be allowed to hang on to any progress I've made. There is no such rule, but I look for it all the same, wasting valuable effort. It is all process. The skills I learn are what stays. For now, there is no practical proof of what I'm learning. What matters is how I can make myself, as the vessel that holds such knowledge, more able to receive the essence of what comes through, without trying so hard to hold on to it. My challenge is trusting that I am doing what I need to do.

After a hot bath, at home with the cats, I feel like I'm about to turn the corner to being less insecure again. Tomorrow starts a new pattern, going to see my therapist on Mondays instead of Wednesdays, going to the job training center the rest of the week. I have retreated too much into my safe hole recently. Changing the pattern will do me good.

A few days into the job skills program, I have a severe headache late in the afternoon and a debilitating fear of collapse. I have a job interview next Tuesday morning. Last night it felt like the ceiling would come crashing in. I went to bed exhausted. In the morning I was able to function better. I took a shower, cleaned the litter boxes, got dressed and dried my hair, played with the cats. Now I feel well.

In class I had the challenge of dealing with someone who wants to get to know me better although I have no inclination to do the same, but I saw the challenge as an opportunity to patiently say No until that person gives up. Her ways remind me of my mother's, so I will do with as little contact with her as I can. I can use the practice in tolerating a situation without saying Yes when I should say No. That is part of the process of drawing boundaries. I did have the impulse to leave and not come back because of this woman, but I didn't give into it, this time. The change is part of the discomfort I feel.

Yesterday I talked to my doctor about the overwhelming anxiety that still comes in waves, as she confirmed for me that dealing with it will be a life-long process, much like having to deal with an addiction. Anxiety has become my default mode, so it's likely to remain an issue. I had mentioned that it's just dawning on me now that there won't be a clear point of distinction of ending old patterns. Waves of insecurity, or even dread, will continue to come. My only course of action is to knowingly tone them down by involving myself less in behaviors that bring them on. I need to knowingly take the blows as they come, to stand my ground as best I can without fighting them, then regroup and prepare for the next rally, trusting that each time the force of any one blow will lessen, as I become more familiar with it. Dr.Low of Recovery talked about *preparing for the inevitable setback*. This is part of it.

While my parents were alive, criticism came from the outside. Now that they're gone 'the tape' is intact within me, I am sorry to find. According to a friend with a similar experience, that tape never really goes away. It is unrealistic to expect it to, or to hope that it will do more than fade. It's not about what is fair or not. Self-destructive behavior will always be the easier path to follow, but the resolve must be there not to follow it, no matter how much I crave it.

Something of essence was damaged when I was twelve, but it might have happened later instead, even without the move to the U.S. My sensitivity was bound to be challenged when I became more aware of my surroundings, here or elsewhere. It's just that it came down on me so completely, at the time. Now it's as if I'm still searching for a reset point to my life, as I go in deeper to heal old wounds. It's hard going, because my life in Romania as a child is now a blur. Leaving Nonna behind, my elder, my guide till then, was a shock I never recovered from. She poured love out to me as always when she did come, but the damage was already done. I was already in survival mode.

I had been pampered and spoiled up to my parents' defection to the West and ultimately to the U.S., but reality would have needed to be presented to me eventually. I can't say with certainty that it wouldn't have caused harm at whatever time and place I became aware of it. I have to let that sink in, that *we know that we don't know*. What is clear to me today, which may hold into the future, is that neither at twelve nor at twenty-two did I get counseling that might have helped. I am getting it now, and that has to be enough.

Being told to comply or to function wasn't enough, when I broke down. I got back up anyway and functioned, but not without losing progressively more faith in what I was presented with as my new life. As much as I understand now that my parents were doing the best they could, my aim can no longer be to gain their acceptance, even posthumously. What had worked for them, bracing themselves for whatever life had to bring and just going forward, did not work for me. That has to be alright now.

They entered survival mode early on, but their nervous systems were less sensitive than mine. Their enemy, the communist regime, was clearer than mine. They recovered after their breakdowns in their early twenties and proved to the world that they could function despite challenges. I didn't. I didn't hate the communists as a child, I didn't even understand what they stood for. I didn't despise any of my former classmates as they were supposed to despise me and my sister, after my parents defected. I had been lucky enough not to despise anyone up to that point. I had been taught by Nonna to respect my parents and others around me, and that's what I tried to do.

For my parents, survival mode was all there was. In that light, it's no surprise that such demands as they had of me were the only behavior they were capable of. And then, for them, life got a whole lot harder on coming to the United States. They knew force and domination, and they used both. As a result, my will did break.

I woke up early this morning with one of the cats, put on my all-time favorite comedy, Trading Places, and got ready for my job interview. I didn't have the anxiety I'd felt the night before, as if I were forcibly pushing myself into the rest of my life. I watched my movie, made and ate breakfast, checked my hair and makeup and what I needed for the day, and got to my appointment on time. I knew what to expect because I'd done my online research about the company, and I went in without expectations, just ready to see it as practice. I won't make it to the second round of interviews, also because it's not work I feel ready for, but that's alright.

The more important thing is that I wasn't paralyzed with fear, that my anxiety from the night before hadn't stopped me from functioning. That is a first. Just getting through that as well as I did was enough. It became a new reset point, which will hold as it needs to, in the future. After the interview I made it to the class in Elizabeth, though very late, and was able to catch up with the computer work that was slated for the day. Another plus. Then I enjoyed the ham and mustard sandwich that was provided and paid attention in the math refresher course. Tomorrow I will be back there to learn more.

There are six weeks altogether to the class, so almost five more to go. We might get snow overnight, marking the true beginning of winter, but I'm not daunted because I have my rubber boots, my shovel and ice scraper from last year. Challenges come as I'm ready to meet them, lately. I get the right encouragement when I need it, and when it's not forthcoming I know to just get myself to the end of the day so that the next day may bring more. I feel like I'm part of something again, part of a process that will work.

It was especially important to get that much clarity from my doctor, about not expecting anything but the need to continue with a concerted effort, since self-defeating language has been my default mode for so long. However it got there, my challenge is to stop trying to make it go away, because by doing that I only make it stronger; just functioning despite it is enough. If it gets to be too much, if I feel overwhelmed, it is alright to do less for awhile, certainly it's alright not to push. Being told that much was very comforting.

Last night I watched another comedy, laid out my interview clothes on the coat rack by the door, took a hot bath and washed my hair, played with the cats and got to bed early, as I do most nights. In the morning my only expectation was to function, and I was able to do it. "One thing at a time" was the only way to approach it, and it worked. Many times it hasn't, but today it did. Now, after dinner and another movie, I'm getting all this down so that the next time I have a setback I will have this as a marker.

After a good second week at the training program, I woke up with a deep sense of inadequacy again today. Last night I went to bed just after seven for the same reason. Just now I did the dishes, ate breakfast, cleaned the litter boxes, took a shower, and put a load in the wash. I am beginning to understand that this insistent lack of confidence may stay with me no matter what I accomplish.

Last year, writing was part of the process of getting past the feeling of inadequacy, so I am writing again this morning, trusting in more of the same. The dull headache that comes with the feeling is not related to medication, that is clear. It is related to my getting in the way of 'negative core beliefs', my 'inner critic.' In the past I have given this inner critic a face, my mother's. Now I realize that, even with both my parents dead, the critic is still there, working hard to "straighten me out," to bring about the complete collapse of my nervous system. That has been my greatest fear, and it seems to be the aim of this critic.

My job is to endure this feeling until it passes, to get to class on time for the next month, to function as well as I can when I'm not in class, to deal with the physical discomfort as it comes while getting just enough distance from it to recognize it. It is important to remember that *the resoluteness of the muscles will overcome the defeatism of the brain.* That works well in the way of doing physical tasks to distract me from the feeling of not being enough.

Does my 'inner critic' really want me dead? I have to call up thoughts of Nonna and her strong, positive image when that question comes up. I am affirming my life step by step, just doing the things I planned to do long ago, or have talked about doing for a long time. By writing, I am challenging the refrain that has been in place for so long, along the lines of "no one will want me, not as a friend or a lover or an employee."

As long as I was able, for twenty-five years up to my mother's death, to see my debilitating moments as part of a curse, I had a clear enemy. At times it felt like it was me against the world. Now, having to realize that my 'inner critic' has lodged itself deep inside, and that attacking it will only do me more damage, I am at a loss as to how to proceed. Even acceptance from the volunteer instructors in the training program is painful. I keep thinking that as they find out I'm bipolar they will shun me, but that hasn't happened.

The fear of being discovered as a failure or an impostor was so strong until a year ago that I tricked myself time and again into thinking I'm not bipolar. Now I find compassion instead, and am at a loss as to how to let that 'inner critic' die down for lack of involvement from the rest of me. I realize that the support of a mate would make a huge difference, as it has in the past, but am weary of trusting in the image anyone who would take on that role in my life would project, rather than presenting who they really are.

With that said, all I have to do today, with all my chores already done, is not die, and not engage in any of my old arrogance or anger. I was able this week to deny someone a favor that would have been an imposition. That was important. I am not responsible for the fate of those who would blame me for their misfortune. I don't have "to bite that hook" anymore. That's probably what has me in symptoms more than anything, this week. I see that I need focus for myself and my recovery and am willing to let others fend for themselves, when in the past I would have needed to make their lives better before I saw to my own needs.

What there is, is more of the process. *Perfection is a hope, a dream, and an illusion.* I can't see myself past this current hurdle, but I am aware that in time I will get past it, even if I need to crawl over it rather than move past it easily. I can't see myself with a renewed will to live coming from within, but I know from experience that it will come anyway. *A thought can bring on a symptom, a thought can take it away.* We need to *do the things we fear and dread to do, to prove there is no danger.* For me right now that is to keep showing up to see my therapist on Mondays and to go to class the rest of the week.

A year ago now I was in the hospital. My cats were home without me. Realizing that much helped me come to my senses, recognizing the need to take care of them. I had a purpose again. In two or three years I will need to be earning my living. That gives me a sense of purpose too, though it brings with it anxiety. I need to build slowly and thoroughly now, not quickly invent the next step, and the next, and the next.

Writing has helped, so I will do that. Most of all, I need to take the blows of my 'inner critic' as they come, even if it means that I have to retreat into my home often, for now. Nonna, God, and The Way are with me. That I know. I just need to see past the pain, again and again. I need to *do motionless sitting,* again from Recovery, and to acknowledge my *fear of the permanent handicap.* I am in symptoms, but *it's not how you feel, it's how you function* that counts.

I am in withdrawal regarding so much behavior based on self-doubt in the past. Part of that has been the fear of making mistakes. The sense of danger has been strong, though I know that *we need to do the things we fear to do to prove there is no danger,* and that we need to *dare to make a mistake.* I notice that when I've made mistakes in class these past two weeks, the feeling of being an utter failure came right away, and that I immediately wanted to run home to hide my shame, but I made the effort to stay despite my symptoms. Today, at home, I feel the need to hide again, but I'm already in my refuge. It's just me and my 'inner critic' and the two cats. There's plenty to eat, the bills are paid, next month's rent is already on its way. I hang on to the thought of trusting in the process of recovery in general.

This time last year I was still thrusting myself outward, seeking help in the only way that had always come through: on a psychiatric ward. I reopened the wound that would not heal. This time my mother wasn't there in the emergency room to show short-lived concern. I opted for the outpatient program I am part of now, thankfully, after my five days in the hospital. I have faced challenges as they've come since then, slowly coming to trust in the process, more than in the past.

Nervous patients hate routine and fear change. That is very true for me. For example, I see the need for me to work, but I'm afraid of messing up. I have Medicaid through the Affordable Care Act, and would stand to lose it if I started earning more than a certain amount. The fear is of doing well in a job for a little while, losing my health insurance, and then losing the job too due to a mental collapse. That goes back to '99, when I felt unable to continue with a job I liked and was good at, after a hospitalization. I wasn't fired but felt I couldn't continue anyway. I retreated to my parents' house and experienced a deep depression for months as I got help, regrouped and went back to school for massage. Now I'm doing something similar by going to this training program, but something still tells me that

I've already lost. I thought the curse was broken with my mother's passing, but I am finding out now that she was only the face I gave to my 'inner critic.'

I've felt that I failed my mother and father, and thus should be made to disappear. What I'm feeling is part of what is called 'parentization', in which a child is made to assume responsibility for one or both parents early on in life. It is important to look at my life from this point of view again, as I did months ago when my therapist first pointed it out. It ties in closely with my 'negative core beliefs' of being a failure and not being enough. On a day like today, when all I see is *gloom, doom and disaster,* it is important to begin to forgive myself for it more, to see that my parents were human, that they survived certain extreme challenges in their lives the best they could, and as a result had unmet needs which were shifted disproportionately onto myself and my sister. Their direct path to accomplishment didn't allow for major mistakes their children might make. My sister did alright, I didn't. I needed help but didn't know how to ask for it, then entered a pattern of dependence in my early twenties which is still in place, complete with self-destructive behavior. I was able to stay clear of chemical dependencies, but my feelings of inadequacy only grew, over time.

Now I face a challenge as great as just surviving my mother literally, or better said, surviving the continual lack of support from her, other than financial. I needed acceptance from her. She couldn't give it. The question is, what is there for me to do now? How to reconcile what is needed from me so that I can function well in the world around me, with my continued lack of self-esteem? When people bring up my accomplishments, I am doubly hit with self-defeat, as if those accomplishments were irretrievably lost. Being reminded of them only makes it hurt that much more.

Yes, I was a good photographer, a good portrait painter, and more recently a good massage therapist, but I wasn't able to make any of it count for my parents in the way they needed it to count, financially. I failed my family in this way. Now there's no one left to prove success to, so what's the point of trying?

I keep forgetting that there's me, too, that being myself is enough of a reason to continue. I have been prompted recently by a healthy inner drive to keep showing up in my world. I've gone ahead and done it through getting back to writing, through getting this training, even simply through celebrating Christmas again this year. But I keep diving into deep loss without knowing how to get out of it. There is nothing to do but learn how. Staying with 'the point of the pain,' as they put it in the grief seminar, is very important, until I've learned how to climb out of it. I have to go through the process, even if it means churning up old pain before I can move forward. I have to learn to forgive myself as I would forgive others.

What I am, though, is more than this pain. I know it even if I don't have proof of it yet. I feel that I don't even want to bother my cats with my deep sorrow, though they show compassion and a willingness to help.

A question that keeps coming up is "What am I doing still alive when I've disappointed so much?" Every time that occurs to me now, it is clear that I need to focus on showing compassion to my own self. Other people can help peripherally, but this key point needs to be addressed by my own self. I need to forgive myself. How can I, though, having done so much harm? I can forgive everyone else, I can even forgive my 'inner critic' as a distorted version of something that might have been useful once, but what way is there for me to forgive myself? Is there such a way? When will I be able to move on, even without having found the answer? I am stuck trying to answer the question, when what I need to do is move on.

There is no set time for grieving, and unresolved grief can compound over time. That holds for me. How can I help myself get through it? One way that comes to mind now is through prayer. If I can see prayer as asking Nonna for help, I can do it. I fall short of being able to acknowledge my faith in ways other than that. I know that I am lost without Nonna's kind of love, and have to hope that I am worthy of it.

Was I worthy, to begin with, of such a great sacrifice on the part of my parents as to start over late in life, as they did? Did my diagnosis of bipolar disorder negate their accomplishment? Was the loss of face irretrievable at that point? Did I disappoint that much? They worked hard to build up their lives; did my mental illness make their lives that much harder? I can't make up for that, though I need to forgive myself for it. Therein lies my challenge.

When a person no longer has any chance at all to make up for something they've done, how do they function? I thought with my mother gone I would no longer feel this lack, but it has grown instead, that much more. All that is left to do is grieve my loss no matter how long it takes, and then move on. Like the boy in Ordinary People, I hung on and did not die, and I have to find a way to forgive myself for it.

My nerves feel raw from dwelling on so much pain. I have successfully dislodged a pattern of retreat from life these past two weeks with the training class, and my 'core beliefs' are not ready to comply. Hence the headaches and the feeling of insurmountable obstacles to overcome. If I can step back from it a little, more will come.

I prayed intensely toward the end of April last year too, when I'd been in bed staring at the ceiling day in and day out for weeks, and help came in the way of volunteering at the self-help center. Now help may come in the way of an office job. First things first, though. I need to move at a sustainable pace. Getting a suitable job is more important than getting a job right away. It has been very important to make a note of how these debilitating feelings of inadequacy come and go.

My father dealt with feelings of inadequacy by retreating into his home, with us. I learned that from him. He kept saying that he only needed his family. He chose to stay away from social occasions, for the most part. My mother complied, though it didn't suit her to be anti-social. After my sister went away to college, the three of us were even more isolated. I stayed close when my turn came to go to school, a year later. For the first semester I commuted into the city, and even after that I came "home" to my parents most weekends.

I didn't know how to detach. My first real time away was the semester I went to study in Paris, in '88. A year later I was diagnosed with manic depression. I'd forgotten how to pray by then. There was little to sustain me. What I've been doing since that first breakdown is to try to piece my life back together.

Retyping my functional resume this afternoon, I became aware of having retreated into my safe haven, this apartment with my cats, to the point of becoming a hermit. Coming to class four days a week has shifted me into a social setting again. *Nervous patients hate routine and fear change,* but change must come, for healing to take place. What I have to be careful about is not to push too much in one direction or the other, but to make my way gently to more contact with the world.

Last year in March and April I was seeing someone I'd only known to say "Hi" to at the library before. I'd become so isolated that I welcomed even the company of someone I didn't know well. Although I broke it off before any physical involvement could take place, I became even more isolated afterward. The medication I'm on now has diminished my physical drive, thankfully, giving me time to approach any potential relationship slowly and cautiously, as opposed to diving into entanglements during manic times.

Much like with work, I can't see myself in a relationship just yet, though I can see a need for it. I have to give it time and trust in the process. My mental health must still be my *supreme goal,* through self-discipline. My actions in general feel stunted, but they will have to do for now. My knee still hurts too, which limits my ability to walk or swim, but I have to trust that in time it will heal completely, and that I will be able to function better overall.

I trust that the people who will read any of my writing will be encouraged to heal too. It is important to stand any pain incurred in the process also for that reason. I, in turn, have drawn faith from the writing of others at crucial times. I know how important it is to have others express what I feel and need to face. Others will be able to tell their own stories when the time comes. It matters, finding one's voice.

Even as demands of the outside world continue to grow, accepting who I am as a valid person is the first step to healthy functioning. The time is almost here for me to seek such far-reaching forgiveness as to allow for my reentering the world actively, not just in short-lived attempts from which I quickly withdraw. I was in a similar place just after my father's death, but I rushed into a relationship right away to distance myself from my mother, whom I saw as a threat. I needed a buffer, although I didn't see the extent of it at the time.

With that threat gone, as I consider things in a more positive light, I will allow myself to suspend disbelief, like we're asked to in movies, to the point of seeing myself reintegrated in social settings that have been daunting in the past. I will picture myself content, socially active, possibly working and in a healthy relationship. I will remember that days as heavy as today will pass, with faith in myself, God, Nonna, and The Way. I will see this dark period giving way to a more fulfilling one.

P_{art} F_{our}

I can now grasp the potency of addiction. I have been addicted to self-deprecating behavior. That, for me, is part of the pattern of reaching manic highs, because the intense depression that comes with putting myself down all the time has always led to manic highs, whether I've been on medication or not. Every time I've accomplished something, I've found a way to discount it, gotten depressed about it, and opened the door to more mania.

In manic times, self-confidence abounds, because without fail I feel then that I count in ways that I cannot bring myself to feel that I count, otherwise. Having reached a manic high once, the pattern of addiction was set. After my first time, I always wanted more. Understanding that much now is important, because changing my behavior as much as I have this past year has gone directly against the flow of these past twenty-five years. I have been experiencing self-destructive loss for so long that it's all I know. That's addiction. My brain chemistry is experiencing withdrawal as a result, because of my change in behavior.

It's painful to me as to any addict to hear that I can change my life now for the better, if only I hold on to my resolve. Allowing for a power greater than myself to guide me is more painful still, because it implies a compassionate omnipresence, one that has been there all along but which I've only let in now. It encompasses forgiveness to such a degree that there is no rock left to hide behind. That brings me back to my first episode in '89. That was the question I was trying to resolve, then: Is God still alive? The only way I came close to certainty as to that at the time was through mania.

I felt that I was divorcing my parents through shifting my faith to God, despite their command to stay put in the pattern I'd known. Like the ugly duckling, I sensed that there was more. I tried to jump to a more inclusive platform of faith and belief, but missed my mark and crashed. After that I tried to return to that moment of possibility again, always falling short. The pattern was set, like any addict's.

What is left to do now is to just keep showing up in my life. Faith in God doesn't have to be a manic goal anymore, though seeing clearly that it once was will take some time. I need to allow for the pain that will come with the shift. Pain already comes with any encouragement from outside. I need to allow for The Way instead of trying to fight it. It will heal me, if I can do that much. And I don't mean that I will no longer be bipolar, as I assumed would happen in the past, if I could just get past criticism in the family. Perhaps most painful of all is the reckoning that to The Way I am acceptable even with a mental illness. I am agreeing, now, to stay put in restraints until the shakes are over, until the waves of withdrawal have passed.

What I haven't counted on is how many waves of withdrawal there are. After the first few, it's okay to reenter the world, with the understanding that there will be more throughout my life, *the inevitable setback* that Dr.Low of Recovery talked about. I thought I was done with those years ago, but that assumption was my downfall, leading to more isolation and finally to the psychotic episode a year ago. What I can hope for now is that the intensity of these waves will diminish in time, to a manageable level, daily.

My pattern has been to destroy my current environment so as to start fresh. Then, as soon as I start fresh, the feeling of inadequacy rushes in again. I have wanted my family's forgiveness and acceptance so badly that I've reinvented my life over and over again, without realizing that seeking their forgiveness and acceptance was less important than finding my own, and God's.

Why has it been so hard to allow thoroughly for certainty of God's existence? Did I borrow my mother's lack of faith? Did I wear down my own faith by staying in a *temperamental deadlock* with her? With perseverance, can my faith be restored through God's love? So much talk of God is daunting until I remember my connection with Nonna. For her, there wasn't any part of life that didn't include God. After she died, I lost that physical reminder of God's presence in my life, and with my first manic episode I reached for it again but crashed and burned.

For all the years since, I've held on to the possibility that I do count only by brandishing this double-edged sword of chemical instability. Only now, and for the past year, have I laid down my weapons and allowed for blow after blow to come from the 'inner critic', without attempting to defend myself anymore. Instead, I've adopted the way to recovery through all the positive means available. Slowly, I've come to allow for less abuse of my time and generosity, but I've done it through isolation, which has ruled out positive interaction along with the negative.

With the job training program and my active job search, I have disturbed damaging patterns actively, which has brought up so much resistance, like a chemical withdrawal. I get little moments of reassurance that I am on the right track, then the defeatism which is so familiar barges in again. I find it difficult to reassure myself at such times. I know that help is standing by, but I see myself as unworthy of it. The one good thing about it is that I can remember times when the sense of unworthiness was stronger, which means that there has been a shift in the right direction.

In the past year I've learned to curb my spending, I've eliminated my debt, and I have chosen to get help instead of continuing to fight my windmills on my own. Now I'm practicing "not biting the hook", not reacting in the same way to behavior that would have set me off in the past. Because of that, I experience withdrawal symptoms every day, and feelings of ease are rare, but I am moving forward with faith, finally. That doesn't mean that my self is no longer broken, but slowly I'm coming to find that I may be able to function even with visible scars. It's possible that someone will want me even with all my faults. Nonna wouldn't turn me away. As long as I can remember that, I will be able to function. The headaches that come with rerouting 'negative core beliefs' and other powerful symptoms will start to die down. *Symptoms lose their validity with daily contradiction.*

Dr.Low of Recovery insisted on a secular approach to recovery, but I can allow my faith in God a larger part in my general recovery now. Again,

I am thinking of God as part of The Way, not of a God of a particular denomination. I don't think Nonna would mind that. In time, I will begin to remember more moments of joy in all the years since that first culture shock at twelve, and the feeling of inadequacy that came with it.

I failed my parents by not living up to their expectations. The more I accept that, the better off I am. When I've accepted that those expectations were unrealistic, I'll be better off yet. Meanwhile it helps to know that there have been addicts who have been able to function for longer than I have. Eventually that will allow me to reenter a social arena. I just need to do it gradually. There's no more need to interact intensely on any level just to prove I'm alive.

Writing has been and continues to be my most useful tool for fixing and reconnecting blown circuits, so I will stay with that, for as long as it takes. Longhand first, then editing as I type, then daring to make it public through publication. That's a healthy pattern.

With time I will notice gradual shifts to less vindictiveness and more forgiveness, much as when a key computer function will finally be allowed for, that of "search and replace," so that failure may be referred to as disappointment, inadequacy may be referred to as something more forgiving, and 'daring to exist' may become more common than not, until "fake it till you make it" won't bring with it the inside track of seeing myself as an impostor every time I remember my qualities.

I need to remember that a suitable job is more important than having something to show for my existence through financial success. For me, for now, that means part-time rather than full-time work, in an office, doing things that require more doing than thinking, so that new patterns of self-worth can take hold gradually. The time is not yet for singing my praises, because compliments still leave me feeling raw. Putting myself out in the world by way of my resume online and through job applications is proving to be daunting, like getting my writing published has been and continues to be. Doing both at a rate I can sustain is as important as doing either at all.

I have hoped that in time I may make a living through my writing. That is not entirely out of the question, but it needs to be alright that it may not happen. It is my process of internal recovery. By reflecting actual events, it allows me to better deal with them. It creates the distance I need to put even things that are very painful in perspective. But I look forward to social interaction through a job, because it turns out that interaction at that level brings new perspective, as well as the opportunity to practice changes in behavior. It just needs to come at a rate I can handle, and for now that rate is the training program, even if it seems that I've got more skills and have accomplished more than other people there. It is for me a more helpful version than the drop-in center, and just as necessary.

What is becoming clear is that there is a path laid out for me after all, because events come as I can handle them, even if I feel daunted consistently. I am not desperate financially, but it's good that I wouldn't wait until such a time as that to reintegrate myself into a functional life. Making the effort now, while I'm not in dire straits, allows for (failure) disappointment with what to others seem like reasonable expectations. Almost a year ago I was desperate in applying for several jobs I wasn't ready for. This is more of that process. It's not getting a job that is the point, it is the reintroduction to social interaction that counts more, which in turn will lead to the ability to hold a job once I get it. It's important to see the difference.

The aim of pushing Quality into coin is there in the program setting, as it needs to be to some extent in any job-seeking enterprise, but I need to establish a firm foundation for it before I can proceed. Working on my resume and applying for jobs online with my job coaches has been part of that. Going through the online publishing process has been part of that too. My experience up to now is the raw material to be refashioned into Quality. It can be done, it just needs to happen at a rate I can manage.

I have always sought teachers and mentors. It's the same now. Learning basic computer programs through the training program not only gives me a sense of accomplishment, it is part of doing wind-sprints, as they called basic training at the start of any athletic season, in the networking group I was part of years ago. It is important to reengage basic functions before moving on to more in-depth training. Doing things gradually is more important than ever. Not fitting into a particular social situation needs not to matter, if I can acquire positive skills as a result of being there. The self-help center turned out to be too much for me to handle as a volunteer facilitator. The current training program has a much better chance for success, precisely because of the factor of instruction and instructors.

Nonna was my elder when I was a child. It is alright to surround myself with teachers I feel could reflect her in various aspects now. That helps rebuild a lasting foundation for more to come, as much as anything. I need it. I've skipped steps too many times in the past, sometimes with very damaging results. It is important to go one step at a time now, catching more errors as I make them and choosing to fix only some of them instead of feeling that I have to be perfect at any one level before going on to the next. That way, the process of growth can return to being positive.

Which brings me to an important realization – growth has meant failure (disappointment) in the past. I've skipped too many steps and tripped or fallen as a result. With the several art shows I had, one seemed to bring more disappointment than the one before, ending in the debilitating return to the East coast, when I'd found a refuge I thought I could keep in Western Canada. Even the pace was different there. The sense of disappointment only grew upon my return, until I went back to school for massage in 2000. I was a good student then, as I have been before in my life, and I had the stamina it took to make it through a whole year of classes and then start work.

This, now, is a version of that. Though the aim is to find work, what is more important is the process. My current insecurities rise out of the fear of being plunged into a job before I've been able to complete the basics, to reset my foundation. That brings on the compulsion to quit, since it's what I know how to do, to sink into helplessness so as to get compassion, because that was the only thing that brought compassion from my mother. She's gone, but the mechanism is still in place. The path is so well-laid, like a super-highway, that it is taking all my strength to insist on not quitting. All my symptoms in this instance relate to this 'negative core belief,' even though I see how much damage it can do, like any addict knows that they might one day overdose if they continue to do their drug of choice.

I need to find a way to safely park the vehicle I've driven for so long, to find my way on foot, at least for now, to slow down my pace overall until I can get back into any level of functioning. If I continue in my old ways now I would be like a race car driver continuing a race that has a higher probability for disaster than normal. The prize, whatever it might be, even of acceptance on a broader scale, isn't worth it. That's why all I need to do for now is seek more balance in my life, by *lowering my expectations so my performance will rise.* Like Dr.Low said, *it's simple but it's not easy.* Eventually, this attitude can bring relief and the ability to function with less interruptions.

A painful realization is that I have been acting out of despair rather than need. I need a job, or an income, for social and financial reasons, but have confused working with personal worth for at least fifteen years. When I stopped working to help take care of my father, I felt that I failed at my purpose when he died in the end. More recently, I felt that I had no further purpose when my mother died. I had been so caught up in our *temperamental deadlock* that I felt responsible for her death. That would confirm that I was a bad daughter, as she always told me I was, and that I should be punished. That's why, even now, I have a *gloom, doom and disaster* attitude. I'm still waiting to get punished.

I have been a desperate person with the attitude of a refugee who is grateful just to have a roof over her head; I have lived with the thought of impending disaster at any point. This past weekend something shifted. I started typing in my current longhand notes since the turn of the year, but stopped at dinnertime, and after dinner I took a bath. Until now, even with my most recent writing, I've felt that I had to get the job done, whatever it was, as quickly as possible, even if it meant agonizing over mistakes later, just to leave something behind in case of a premature death.

I couldn't help but notice, recently, that I've approached my job search in the same way, out of desperation. I've needed to show that I want to become worthy, to be approved of. My family in the past had been thoroughly disappointed – I needed to prove them wrong now, even if only through a sheer effort of the will. That is desperate behavior, and what I've come to realize is that through this approach I am bound to always be in more symptoms. Besides that, I am bound to uphold my work pattern in the past, of being discouraged with my imperfect output to the point of quitting before I got fired. It was always important to take any job that was offered, even with massage, initially, to overlook an uncomfortable fit at first, with the aim of making it work, making it fit.

My father spent his last month in a facility, because my mother and I were no longer able to cope with him at home. After his death, I knew that I didn't want to be my mother's caregiver, something she took for granted would happen. To avoid that, I entered a relationship right away, without taking the time to realize that it might drain me as much in the end. When that relationship ended, I felt I'd failed again, and treated attention from men that entered my life as a temporary distraction. My mother had moved back to Romania by then, so I was unhindered to pursue my career in massage therapy. But the pattern had been set in place so concretely, of seeking worth through accomplishment, that any criticism from my family resulted in self-deprecating behavior. I wanted to succeed, but felt unworthy of success.

In '99 I wasn't fired from my job even after a manic episode, but I quit because being found out as a manic depressive was too much to bear.

It's difficult even now to disclose to any potential employer that I'm bipolar, in part because I fear not getting hired or being fired soon after I sign on, but on the other hand I need it to be alright that I am bipolar. I need validation from an outside source so badly, but I feel doomed to disappoint from the start because I disappointed my family so thoroughly when I was first diagnosed.

Whenever I accomplish something now, even privately, like through writing, my 'inner critic' is there to remind me of what a failure I really am. It is only faith in The Way which allows me to pick myself up every time. It seems that I can gain self-respect only inch by inch, and at the expense of severe symptoms. That has to be alright, since it is what it is: a part of the process of recovery.

Last night it felt like I gained a foot rather than an inch, after a weekend of symptoms. I didn't feel the terror of having to type in all my notes right away even if it were to take all night, as if the world might end otherwise. Until this weekend I'd approached writing as the one weapon I could bear in my fight for recognition as a valid human being, with my family as antagonist. What came through instead, finally, was that not any one book would ensure my victory, that it's not about victory at all. That it's about adopting new positive patterns at a rate that I can handle. That I will continue to write and that writing will continue to help, whether I see myself as a writer or not. Even if it turns out that I am one, it is alright to have a job in "the real world" to support me financially.

When I first started writing, what came up strongly was that either there was a God, who would provide me a path to an income as an artist, or there would be a little job somewhere for me to take as I buried my head in the sand and stayed there. It's only dawned on me recently that this black-and-white approach has stayed in place for so long.

As I finished Cooper, my parents wanted me to come back to live with them in Cranford and work at a one-hour photo shop. They were planning to "straighten me out." That would have meant failure for me at the time, after considerable waves of creativity at school. I hadn't taken a job in the advertising field a year before because my parents had insisted that I finish school and get my degree. Now they wanted me to settle for what I saw as menial work. After my first hospitalization, that first week of May 1989, any job seemed unattainable.

More importantly, there was the issue of God's existence. He was my private mentor, I felt; as his pupil I felt empowered to continue to pursue art as my means of validation. I fought my 'inner critic' with Him as my shield. It didn't occur to me at the time that any such God who might encourage a crusade was one of my own making, despite my feeling that I was part of a more inclusive Way which has never been about conflict other than as its resolution.

For that reason, for many years, a job seemed a defeat, as opposed to a career. Now comes the challenge of both trusting in God and The Way, and at the same time finding worth in that job that will pay the bills. It will be a part-time job to start, with skill requirements I can match. I can allow for the time it will take to find the right job now, as I adjust out of my desperate ways.

For a year now, I've spent money cautiously, I've paid off my debts, and I've sought to simplify my needs. All of this has allowed for reflection through writing again, creating a bridge to potentially sustainable work for the first time. I don't need to start painting again to feel worthy this time, as much as I value my skills as an artist.

I've thought of writing as therapy for twenty years, not as an art form. The distinction has allowed for continuing with it, instead of casting it off along with other artistic pursuits. Over time, I've left enough traces through my writing to create a real lifeline for whenever I need it. Now I can conceive of also reclaiming my sense of humor, which will help bring about a more lasting sense of security. As Dr.Low said, *humor is our best friend, temper is our worst enemy,* and *we can have only secure thoughts or insecure thoughts at any one time, never both.* That means that if I can plant a secure thought for myself even while in severe symptoms, I have already partially dislodged any sense of doom. And that's what I've been doing.

Resting adequately and eating well, resisting the impulse toward desperate behavior, has worked, even if, or especially because, more daunting symptoms crop up as a result. I am hanging in there, storm after storm. On a morning as good as this one I can see worth in it. I thought I had nothing left to prove when my mother died, but it turns out that there will always be a residual need to prove something, if only to myself. Integrating that need into more practical ones is part of my challenge.

In the meantime, it keeps coming to mind, my being so alone. Yesterday it came up while we went over the need to network while looking for a job. At the outpatient program they talk about socialization. On the psychiatric ward they made a point of having everyone go to group therapy. I have only the two cats and myself, my therapist and my psychiatrist. In the past five years or so I had social contact through my work.

What is important to note is that while my mother was alive all I knew was to not let her influence me into complete isolation. I used work as a means of combating her negativity. I had been reacting and little else. She took up a lot of space in my life, even from far away. With her gone, what was surprising was the daunting void that ensued.

Now I am alone, but in a way that leads to introspection and healing. I need not to confuse that point. The earth must be allowed to replenish itself for some time after being thoroughly drained. Only then can planting start again. I have to trust that solitude is what I need, for now. As my attitude in general becomes more positive, I will begin to draw people to me who will encourage me to open up more. It's very important not to rush the process.

A few weeks ago there was a mist late into the morning. It was a Wednesday, I remember, because I was going to the out-patient center and I remember editing the pictures I took with my cell phone just before Women's group. I love the soupy feel of mist. Today the snow has been coming down so hard since midnight last night and it's blowing so hard that it's as if it were mist instead snow. I cleaned off my parking spot this morning. If it keeps going this way, I'll have to do it all over again tomorrow. By the time I came back in, the door to the lobby almost wouldn't open from so much snow.

In the windows, layers of snow have set like in Christmas cards. I heard some of my neighbors, including a couple of little kids, laughing out loud in the hallway and then just outside the front door. My light feelings matched theirs. Now all is quiet again. Vinny is napping in the bedroom and The Kiddo is keeping me company here in the living room.

Some of my neighbors have cleaned off their cars too, doing *part-acts*, like me. That's another Recovery *spotting*, doing things in *part-acts* instead of waiting and having to do the task later with that much more effort. It also applies to dealing with symptoms, so that one doesn't get overwhelmed like in the past.

The snow has settled oddly on the cars that haven't been touched, unevenly, molded by wind and more wind. I am grateful for my warm secure apartment. I have been wondering about the stray cats I know of in the neighborhood, hoping that they've been able to make or find shelter.

Here comes Vinny, to investigate the state of affairs. He has a wonderful way of gently tapping my lower back with his paw through the back of the chair as I sit at the computer, reminding me of his priorities. That will come later. For now, he is drinking water out of the heavy glass on the floor which has been their water receptacle of choice for the past year. Soon he will settle into another nap, but not yet. The Kiddo watches, as I turn to look at her. She pays attention to the neighbors through the door. They are by the front door of the building again.

A blizzard like this one is an event. When I've asked random people if they remember last year's season starting off much the same way, most of them have said that they didn't remember anything but snow and more snow. Last week there was a dusting. This is different.

Vinny is watching it now, from the windowsill. He hasn't left the apartment since he moved in except to go out into the hallway, and I sometimes wonder if he's aware that the world outside is an extension of the world inside, and the other way around. Several times I've said hello to him from outside through an open window, as I was going to my car, but I'm not sure he knew it was me. Sometimes we hear the strays howling, at intervals, and both he and The Kiddo show concern, so I know he hasn't entirely forgotten his days as a stray, but it was so long ago that the memory must be very remote. I am extremely grateful for their presence, for being allowed to notice them in their daily comings and goings, and for being the one who takes care of them.

Light is starting to fade outside, but the snow keeps coming. Last year at this time I'd been out of the hospital for only a couple of days, had paid my bills and my rent and ordered some books from a place in Princeton. As the medication settled in more, I stopped that kind of extraneous spending, though it seemed important, at the time. The books I bought then are safely in the closet. They replaced the ones I'd blacked out ISBN numbers in. I don't need to understand why it seemed so necessary to me at one time to not have my books easily identified through their ISBN. I was slowing down the pace of automation in general, I thought. Now I have a healthy respect for how my thoughts can drift into a parallel mode, without medication. It took some time to get the new "cocktail" right, but it was worth it.

Both cats are now on the sill, and back down again. They each have their favorite chair. The Kiddo goes to have a closer look at the shovel and the brush by the door, then retreats to the bedroom. Vinny follows her. Here she comes back again, stopping by the sofa to lick herself clean. She is the bigger and stronger of the two, but Vinny is still the one who intimidates. The Kiddo's mother was fostered in the same home as Vinny. Maybe she doesn't realize that, once grown, her behavior toward Vinny could change. Here he comes to my chair again, to remind me that I should be cuddling with him on the sofa, while watching a movie.

After an hour's cuddle, it's time to stretch again. I am getting a feeling today that I haven't had before, that things will be alright, in time. It isn't something that I had to talk myself into, as I've done before. It's just an easy feeling, like I belong in my life.

Yesterday, at the class on building job skills, several good things happened. I applied online for a job that would suit me, I felt comfortable joking with the volunteer instructors present, and I helped one of my classmates with an online application. The job I applied for was doing reception for a senior citizen home. I mentioned in my cover letter that I'd helped look after both my parents towards the time of my father's death, and writing about it gave me a sense of accomplishment. I tried my best with them, I came to realize. Whether I get the job or not, I was able to see that time as a positive marker.

The instructor who proofread my cover letter said she wouldn't change a thing. That compliment settled well over one that the retired English teacher paid me the day before, on a practice cover letter. He said that anyone who would read that letter would hire me because I know how to write a letter well. It felt like I had something to contribute again. Tonight, as the blizzard keeps at it outside, I am well, here at home. I watched part of Scent of a Woman again with Vinny stretched out along my side; now I'm putting notes directly into the computer for the first time, skipping the step of writing longhand first. I wanted to see if I could, and it's coming easily.

In class, I had to stare at the page for awhile, but thankfully the English teacher had provided a template. That, and the gentle encouragement of whichever angel is looking after me today, made me remember the scene in Finding Forrester where Sean Connery's character gets his young protégé going with a paragraph of his own, to start. I feel protected and loved, here with my two cats in my living room. I have worked really hard lately at becoming more of a human being, and it feels like it's coming. Not there just yet, but not far off. I count too.

About a week ago I watched Scent of a Woman after about a year's break, and it still blew my mind, the same as before. I have felt that alone too. Thinking of how good an actor Al Pacino is, brings me right back to John Travolta going on about him on film, a short time before John Travolta too became big. That brings me to Get Shorty, with a seasoned John Travolta turning on the charm in Hollywood. That's how my mind works, through association. I'm happy not to know about my favorite actors' personal lives. What they put across on film is enough.

What is it that I put across? Can't be all bad if I can feel comfortable joking with the volunteer instructors in the job skills class. The day before yesterday, after the cover letter lesson, there was the first of four lessons on Powerpoint. I panicked, looking at the printout that came with it, but the instructor was so reassuring and made it so clear that, in the first lesson at least, we were supposed to have fun, that I relaxed. The anxiety was intense for that first ten minutes, as if I was about to fall flat on my face, but I didn't run. It was as if I were learning a different language again, like that first two months, thirty-six years ago, when I couldn't understand what any of my classmates were saying at Orange Avenue School, halfway through seventh grade. I think it was then that I started skipping steps instead of giving each one time to settle. Eventually I understood what people were saying, and have loved the English language since, but the initial sense of inadequacy then still comes up, now and at intervals, to the point of my wanting to run and hide.

That's how one positive experience can place a positive marker or establish a reset point in a way that no mental effort alone could do. Getting through something difficult is different than conceiving of doing it. They say to "see yourself in the job" when preparing for an interview. Yesterday with the senior citizen center job was the first time I could see myself fitting right in, because of my old-fashioned respect for elders. That's opened the door for my seeing myself in a life beyond what I have now. It allowed for the possibility of a more permanent home, maybe with a mate who won't run and whom I won't have to run away from. I didn't even have to cry about it, tonight. It's Saturday night, there's a blizzard out, in a few days it will be my forty-ninth birthday and I don't have any plans, but I'm at ease in a way I've only hoped for, before. Trusting in the process has allowed for it, trusting in God, Nonna and The Way.

The other thing I can count on is having Vinny wake me up around six-thirty every morning. Pretty soon, when my knee finally feels up to it, I will be able to use that early morning prompt to get to the pool for a few laps. Going to bed early is alright. I've kept up my membership at the Y these past few months since I strained my knee, thinking I'd go back to swimming in the afternoons, but my life is getting busier and Vinny is consistent in his early morning timing, so I'll give an early morning swim a try. I still have my old suit and my cap, which will come in handy now that my hair is growing in nicely.

What I see happening consistently is that I am able to manage better on my own. Having survived a difficult period in my life, it is alright to get support in rebuilding a social life. Three weeks of the class have already passed, there are three left, and I can *anticipate joyfully or not at all* that I will become more at ease in general by the end of the sixth week. All I've done is to consistently show up in my life, to ask for help where appropriate, and something has shifted.

This afternoon one of my mother's more caustic comments came to mind, but I was able to let it go right away. That was a good sign. Practicing harmlessness is no longer a goal, but a reality. It becomes clear that whatever damage was done to my self-esteem can be undone, with just more of the same: eating, sleeping, playing with the cats, showing up when and where I said I would. Something has given way. It doesn't have to be as daunting to function anymore. Whatever tools are no longer functional will be replaced with better ones, one by one, and my life will be mended. Like with an old-fashioned eraser going over an old-fashioned chalk board, things can be allowed to slip away from the forefront for the time being, until they don't stand out as much as wrong or painful.

We made it through the storm, but the roof caved in on my favorite food store in a neighboring town. I found out about it from one of the people in my building while I was doing laundry next door. The laundry room in the basement wasn't open. Like other people, I suspect, I took it for granted that I'd stop in at the store for some of my staples in the next couple of days, and make small talk about the storm with the person at the checkout counter. Now there's just a collapsed building where I was used to so much activity. I'd had a little ritual of parking a few blocks away and walking, sometimes stopping at my favorite thrift store on the way back. It will take some getting used to, not doing that anymore. Change always does. I had a hard time when the health food store closed last summer, too. Eventually I stopped looking at the For Lease sign in the window as I passed.

I had to shovel for over an hour again today. The plow had packed in feet of snow in front of my car. I took my time and got it done. Then I walked around to the back of the building and saw how little had been cleared. In places, the snow was four feet deep, and other cars were buried as much as my car had been, and more. By the time I looked again in the afternoon, it was much better. Tomorrow I need to go see my therapist at the out-patient center. I'll bring my shovel, just in case.

It occurs to me that I saw the storm as an adventure, from my safe haven. Now I'm more grateful than ever for what I have. I will adjust to having to shop elsewhere for my essentials, but every time I will shop elsewhere I'll remember the caved-in roof, for awhile, and think of the impermanence of what I take for granted. There's no sensationalism in it, but it does matter.

I will have to work on not owning situations that are out of my control. Almost right away I put myself in the shoes of someone I know who worked there, thinking that he will now have to collect unemployment until he finds another job. It's not for me to worry about; I'm sure he'll land on his feet, and yet I find myself feeling as vulnerable as he might be feeling right now. If anything, I am reminded that I attach too much importance to other people's hardship and am quick to wonder if there was something I could have done about it.

Somewhere in the parking lot a car is beeping its horn insistently. That probably means that their parking space was taken by someone who doesn't belong there. This morning, as I was cleaning off my space I was counting my blessings, with my own secure spot. When I'd lived in Clark there was never a guarantee that the spot I'd shoveled out wouldn't be taken when I got home. On top of that, the heating and cooling bills were always high because the walls were thin. Where I live now utilities are included, and my cats are allowed.

I continue to be apprehensive at times about how vulnerable I am without someone to count on in emergencies, but then I remember that there are *possibilities and probabilities.* It is possible that I won't be able to cope when something unexpected occurs, but the probability is that I'll do just fine. Remembering that much allows me to break the cycle of worry early on. It still surprises me to have Recovery *spottings* come to mind as I need them, despite the fact that it's exactly what Dr.Low meant to have happen. *Trigger symptoms require trigger spotting.* The method of gaining reassurance through will-training works, I'm glad to be able to say.

It's not how you feel, it's how you function comes to mind for tomorrow. It'll be the first time I'm out driving in snow-covered roads this year. Three weeks ago I had to adjust to having to find parking near the church where the job skills class is being held. I did alright with that, but only through perseverance. Tomorrow I will be a few blocks away from the church, at the out-patient center. Sometimes there's parking in the hospital parking lot so there's less need to worry; I know that but I notice anxiety cropping up anyway.

The same person is still honking the horn. I catch myself entering that person's shoes. It happened to me once too but the guy responsible for it came out right away. Besides, it was summer and I could easily have parked a block away if I'd needed to. Whoever this is probably doesn't have the energy to shovel out another space tonight. There goes the horn again. Technically the car that is at fault could get towed. That brings to mind a memory of a friend who'd parked in the snow around the corner and had his car towed because it was too close to the edge of the drive. That was my one experience with how towing happens locally.

I would love to have a human to share my concerns with. That way mountains could be reduced to molehills more easily. My cats have a calming effect, especially because they take their cues from me. If they are calm, as they are tonight, it is a direct reflection of me. I'm glad to be able to say that and have it be true. Still, it would be nice to have someone to call for reassurance. In time, even that may come. For now, I reassure myself by counting all the positive aspects of my life, "checking the facts", like my therapist says.

The car stopped honking the horn, so that situation has been resolved, one way or another. In time the memory of it will fade, grouped with tonight's concerns. In the meantime it's important to just keep showing up in my life. There is only so much caution a person can adhere to. Today I did my laundry, tomorrow I will run my errands in my rubber boots. I used them for all the shoveling, and was dry and comfortable in them. Then, to go to the laundromat, I wore my little boots and felt the water come in right away through the seams along the sole. At least I'll know now not to wear them if I'm going to be walking through puddles.

I even took a hot shower and soaked my knee in Epsom salts after this morning's shoveling. That should make a difference for tomorrow. There is nothing more than this for now, being with my cats, managing moments of anxiety, functioning as well as I can. I will need to get more orange juice and mineral water tomorrow. I've been eating well and sleeping well. I already took my meds for tonight and am slowly getting groggy. It's a day for counting all the positive things I've done. The fitting Recovery spotting is *when we're endorsing ourselves we're not blaming ourselves.* I remember a time when I didn't need so much reassurance, when I lived in Canada, but life is what it is, so going through the recovery process day by day is key now. Writing helps.

Today, what changed was my attitude. *If you can't change the situation, you can change your attitude toward it.* I had plenty of anxiety to start, so I did things in *part-acts* again to get myself going. After taking care of the cats, giving them their morning treats and cleaning their litter boxes, I took out the garbage and went for a walk to the side road and back to get an idea of how best to leave the parking lot. By the time I got back, the choice was made: I had to exit directly into the main road, which I generally avoid because too often there are cars parked alongside, blocking the view. But today there were no cars on the road. The entrance off the side road would be manageable when I returned, too.

After getting myself ready, I called the bank to see if the right person was there to handle a transfer of funds to my sister. She wasn't, but someone else could take care of it, I was told. I had enough time to go do that and then make it to my appointment with my therapist in Elizabeth, so I ventured out.

Driving into Cranford, I noticed that the snow had settled deep there too. It was logical that it would, but seeing it for myself made it real. For once, I parked in the municipal lot. I had brought quarters with me, but the pay stations were still blocked by feet of snow. At the bank, I forgot to ask for cash from my account because I was too busy trying to get the transfer off to my sister. It turned out that person who might have helped me hadn't been with that particular branch long enough to do the task, so I was asked to come back in the afternoon. They were very polite about it, I was very polite back.

Coming all the way into the center of town meant that I would be going into Elizabeth down the main road all the way, which wouldn't be blocked, at least not as much as the back roads I would normally take. As I drove I became more and more grateful for my safe parking spot by my building. I kept passing mounds of snow with cars stuck in them.

As I was coming into Elizabeth, at one point the row of cars I was in had to go single-file down a two-way street because there was so much snow around the parked cars that had nowhere to go. Everybody was very patient. Then, nearing the hospital, it became obvious that I wouldn't find parking on the street. My one chance would have been to find a spot open in the outpatient program parking lot, or in the hospital lot. I kept going with that intent.

On either side of the road, I noticed people putting chairs into the road to claim spots that had been cleared. I remembered that last year my therapist had mentioned that it's an accepted practice to do that here, after a snow storm. There was something very natural about it, since that came to mind. I'd never seen it anywhere else. It's part of a community code.

More people than usual were waiting for the bus at the corner of Broad and East Jersey. More people than usual were in the street, it seemed to me. Everybody had somewhere to go. Then, nearing the hospital, there were more chairs in the open spots.

I made it to the out-patient center, but there was no parking to be had. It was already after ten-thirty. Normally even on a regular day there are few spots left by the hospital by then. I pulled into the hospital lot, which was also full, and called my therapist. She was there. It turned out that her car had been snowed in at home, so she took the bus into Elizabeth. As usual, she spoke in a calm and reassuring way. I told her where I was and that I wouldn't be able to make it, that I would call her later. Then I started on my way back. I already had in mind to stop at the Roselle Park library, to call in again from there. I took another way back this time, to avoid the strait I'd come in through. I felt proud of myself for knowing there was more than one way to get home.

When the time came, I turned right to go toward the library. Their parking lot had been cleared. I guessed from it that the lot at the Cranford library must have been plowed out too. I parked and called my therapist again. She was still there, and we did a twenty-five minute session by phone. I told her about the roof falling in on that building in Westfield, about my concern for the people who worked there in general and that one person I'd gotten to know a little in particular. We talked about how good it is that I can at least see that I'm taking on responsibility for things I can't help; identifying patterns like that is half the battle.

I was warm in my car and had remembered to pack the battery charger for my phone, which was running out of power. I *endorsed* myself for that too, and made a mental note to leave home with a fully charged phone, next time, though it was comforting to see that the USB connection worked. It didn't work in another car I'd had. So, after patting myself on the back for getting to the library safely, for talking to my therapist and having gained some more confidence, I thanked her for being there for me and moved on.

She'd looked up the bus line that could bring me to Broad Street in downtown Elizabeth, this coming week of classes. She'd even looked up the intersection I could catch it at, in Roselle Park. She'd walked the half hour to the hospital from Broad Street herself. I did that once too, the very first day I was due at the out-patient center, having confused another affiliated building with it. We talked about how important the job skills class has become. In the aftermath of the storm, we were finding ways for me to continue with it, given the current hurdle.

I wasn't due back to the bank till after noon, so after the talk with my therapist I made my way into Cranford at an easy pace, planning to go into the Cranford library to do more research on my potential bus trip. As I got close to it, however, it turned out that the lot hadn't been touched yet. Several cars were in the lot, deep in snow up to the windows. First I thought how surreal it was to see these marooned cars, then I worried about their owners. Again, I was assuming responsibility for something that was completely out of my hands. I made a note of it, and repeated to myself what my therapist had said, that noticing the behavior is important in itself. Then I turned the corner, minded my way, and headed for the bank.

The person I needed to see at the bank was busy. I was glad I'd packed my quarters, because the pay stations in the municipal lot were now accessible. A space opened up just as I was pulling in. I got cash out of my account and went across the street to get some decaf coffee and a croissant. The person behind the counter remembered me, although I hadn't been there in months.

At the bank, I'd noticed one of the people I knew worked at the store that had caved in. I told him that I was sorry and asked how he was. He was very polite and asked my name, told me his. After I left, it occurred to me that I'd been compelled to say something, so that I could let it go. It was a nice interaction. I was reassured that there was already a plan underway to rebuild.

I sat there in the coffee shop thinking about it, while they were brewing my fresh cup of coffee. When the coffee was ready, I dunked my croissant in the coffee cup at leisure, took my time eating and drinking, and left without saying good-bye. The person who had served me was busy with another customer, so it was alright to not do that. It occurred to me that I give too much importance to casual behavior, mine included.

When I got back to the bank, the person I needed to see was still helping someone else. I remembered that I'd put enough quarters in for an hour, so there was no rush. The first business day after a major storm it's good to make allowances. I settled into a comfortable chair and waited. Soon she was able to take me and we took care of the transaction without much ado. I had called my sister to let her know about the transfer in the morning, so I wanted to make sure to get it done the same day. Once it was done, all I had left to do was go food shopping.

I was more careful than usual on my way to the store. It seemed like everyone was being more careful than usual. Pulling into the small lot, I noticed that people were doing their best to function well just as much as I was. A large supermarket closed in the area around Thanksgiving, so this one has been getting that much more business. There were no complaints about the twenty or so spaces that weren't available because snow had been plowed into them to make the rest of the lot available. People seemed to be functioning efficiently inside too, both as customers and employees. We were all grateful to be there, I think. At least I was. I filled my basket and checked out at the automated teller, as usual, then made my way carefully out to the parking lot. It was just above freezing, so the black ice had melted.

I had no trouble pulling in at home, and backed into my space with the driver's side window open. I got distracted and left it open when I went inside, but half-an-hour later one of my neighbors knocked at my door to let me know I should go close it. I didn't beat myself up for it, but I did remember right away that I'd knocked over my cats' favorite water dish in the morning. My pattern of adding negative events together and not noticing the positive is still strong. That is partly why I'm going through the whole list of events now, to knowingly downplay it. I remembered instead that I had refrained from taking a call while driving, which was important since I couldn't have pulled over even if I'd wanted to.

When I got home, I checked in with the cats and then looked at my message. It was the class organizer letting me know there wouldn't be class tomorrow. I looked up the schedule to see what we would miss and noticed that in two days we're supposed to go to the thrift store in Cranford, where a benevolent group of volunteers helps clothe low-income women for a professional look. It's a part of the class that has been in place for years. So, more to be grateful for. That, and my cats being as welcoming as ever.

As we often do, the cats and I took a nap in the afternoon. Then I came into the living room to warm up my dinner and jot down some notes. It's past eight o'clock now and the building staff are still working on clearing areas of snow. I can hear them backing up at intervals. My cats are curled up comfortably on their chairs, neighbors come and go in the hallway; it's been a good day. I had wondered in the morning what my anxiety was tied to, but in the end it didn't matter. It was more important to function. Luck was with me, I made it through each part of the day, got home safe and can look forward to staying put tomorrow. It mattered, that I was willing and able to downplay anxiety. In the past I would have been afraid to go out at all. *We are a capable and courageous lot but we paralyze ourselves with fear*. What was helpful to consider was the need to have patience with things that went wrong. All in all, it was a good day.

It occurs to me this morning more than ever that I am protected and loved. I ask for help and it comes. So what is my anxiety about? It continues to crop up, even as I back up from it to get a clearer picture. If nothing else comes to mind, I find myself worrying about how my hair looks.

I stay with the feeling of insecurity to let it die at its own pace. My 'inner critic' questions the writing I'm doing. What am I trying to prove, it whispers. I tell it that since I've gotten encouragement about it lately I will go ahead and do it more. Monks are taught to not expect enlightenment through achievement, but to eat when hungry and sleep when tired, to forget about the active search for a state that cannot be grasped by an effort of the will. For me, there's also the need to write, when the opportunity comes.

I have been drawn to the writing of elders who know bits and pieces of the whole experience of enlightenment. It's what I was shooting for in my last year of college. My father wanted me to become an instant financial success, I was trying for what might make life bearable when all I saw around me was material pursuit. I had no distance from what I was doing at the time, so my fall from grace was harsh, with my first hospitalization.

In yoga they talk about the sleeping serpent at the base of the spine, which, when awakened abruptly, instead of at the right pace, can wreak havoc. That holds for me. My nervous system was short-circuited. I've come to understand that such an explanation doesn't fly in the face of logic, or doesn't have to. It can work with the diagnosis of manic depression. Artists and musicians over time have had to face similar questions.

I realize that I am still in the process of accepting my illness as such, because I continue to have regret about so much destruction over time. It is only starting to sink in that recovery for me couldn't have taken another course. I was busy just surviving for so many years, incurring more and more damage just to keep going.

In manic times I had no problem feeling a part of things, which is what I craved. Now this sense of belonging is coming in more comprehensive waves rather than in spurts. The right medication has brought a balance I'd given up on. In time, if I can ever afford it, I would like to get CranioSacral treatments. That is a form of massage that addresses the fluid that coats the spinal chord and brain. I took one class in it six years ago and saw the value of it right away; I even wanted to find a mentor to teach me the method one-on-one. It didn't happen, but I still look forward to the time when it might.

I can allow for the possibility because certain pursuits have manifested in my life in cycles, so CranioSacral massage might too. I intend to officially close up shop as a massage therapist this year, but the skills I've learned over these many years doing it will stay. In the context of job-hunting it makes sense to return to doing massage, at first, but if I consider my overall health, including my damaged right knee and shoulder, it doesn't.

I notice that I've approached massage therapy overall as an apprenticeship. It seems that's what I do, while still seeking a mentor who might render me into more. It's not a practical pursuit but it helps with understanding what motivates me. I've returned to writing as an apprenticeship too, after a three-year break, first blurting out feelings about my mother again, now by going back to the basics through observation. It now occurs to me that The Way, which for me includes God and Nonna, has been guiding me all this time. I know I am not enlightened, but I am no longer separate from The Way, either. I no longer feel blasphemous thinking of myself as not separate from God. I feel I belong as part of God's manifestation on Earth, as much as the trees outside my window. They have lost their leaves for the winter but in the spring they will regenerate, as I might also, when more ease enters my life.

Part of the trick for me will be to let it sink in that the ease that is needed is not financial ease. That I already have, compared to many, though I don't feel I deserve it. After all, I was told I was a bad daughter enough to believe it, and proving myself otherwise is not easy. My 'inner critic' has soaked up the "evidence" of my wrong-doing, and is very reluctant to let go of it. And yet that is what needs to happen.

What will help is to remember that my mother denied any connection she might have had with God. She lived her life partly to make sure things went her way, through material proof of success. As I step back from this observation, I notice that Nonna, her mother, loved her and stood by her anyway, because that's what mothers do. My mother tried to love me but it came out wrong, being all about control through money. It's only occurring to me now that I've had a need to have had Nonna love me more than she did my mother. That means that I've still been competing with my mother, beyond her death. It is important for me to know that Nonna didn't give up on her, just as she didn't give up on me.

Nonna was wise and knew how to show compassion. She is guiding me now in a compassionate way to let go of more pain related to my life as it has turned out. A master of harmlessness doesn't take sides. Until now, I have thought that Nonna did that for me, because I needed an ally in my fight with my mother. Since the time has come for me to walk away more from any final combat, I needed to have that realization, and it has come. In this light, a day at home becomes something else: an opportunity. As one of the job coaches in the job skills class said, every problem can be turned into an opportunity. I asked for help an hour ago, and it's here.

Writing won't make me a good daughter, in fact it's one of the things my mother didn't want me to do, but maybe to someone other than my mother I wouldn't have to prove being good, as much. Maybe in time the inside can match the outside, like a friend said. I kept correcting volunteer instructors in the class when they said I didn't belong there, that with the skills I have I should already have a job. The social setting, I said, was what I need for now. Without such interaction I would be easily daunted by any potential job. What's on paper doesn't match the insides, yet. The class is part of therapy, for me. I need to be reintroduced to being around others.

With the storm this weekend, there are new challenges (opportunities.) I've decided not to take the bus when the class resumes, because half-an-hour walks to and from where the bus would drop me off would be too much for my knee, realistically, even with a brace. So I will splurge and call a taxi. After all, the class is free. The least I can do is contribute the car fare for as long as I need to, until the roads have been cleared and I can park my own car safely again. Giving myself that freedom works. Paying for the oil change instead of taking my car to the dealership gave me freedom too. I addressed the issue *at its weakest link,* and it worked. The highway the dealership is on always makes me nervous, and to take the car there I would've had to wait till the oil level had dropped to fifteen percent. It was just a little above that, and with the storm coming I didn't want to take a chance. My training in Western Canada told me that the precaution was worth taking.

I notice that in the past year I've started a new positive trend: when I have to deal with a problem I stop and consider it from a distance, as much as time allows, and I ask for advice when I feel stumped. Some of my nerve endings still feel raw when I remember rash reactions and manic spending, as if I should be trying to undo what was done because otherwise I will disappoint. I have assumed stigma is there, whether it is or not. *Stigma is the last to go,* and one's own stigma hangs in there indefinitely, in fact it overlaps with one's 'inner critic'. There is no point trying to eradicate it, because it is as tough as weeds that come up through cracks in the pavement. Pouring weed-killing compound on it isn't an option either, because it contaminates the soil. In this light, taking a taxi into Elizabeth for the class is not a luxury, it is an appropriate solution. Tomorrow I will call up the local cab company to set it up.

I am reminded briefly of the car services I used in Brooklyn in '99, with the boyfriend I had at the time. I don't remember the details, but the memory reinforces for me that sometimes what seems like a luxury is actually a need. When I left him I took the subway, I remember, with just a handbag and my cat in the cat carrier. She was a very wise gentle cat I'd adopted at a farmer's market. I was going all the way back to Cranford, and would have to keep her separate from my parents' cats, in the basement.

She was very calm on the subway. I opened the lid of the carrier and she let herself be petted, very much at ease. As it turned out, my ex-boyfriend passed on a message days later that a job I'd applied for months earlier was open for me to take, and I found another apartment in Brooklyn shortly after beginning at my new job.

The Way was looking out for me then too, but I didn't see it. I was still very much entangled in my difficult relationship with my parents and wasn't taking medication, which was an especially bad combination. It wasn't until the year 2000, when I started therapy in earnest, and stumbled onto Recovery, that I had a real chance as to how to begin rebuilding.

As I jumped from stone to stone, back then, and more recently into my current home, I always felt that something, or someone, was chasing me from behind. Until my mother died I didn't realize that I'd been living like a refugee all along, when I was telling others around me that I was well. This apartment had become my last refuge.

What I've done in the last year has been to make little gains one by one and hold on to them. I've been so isolated that it's been important not to push for more. *There are no uncontrollable impulses, only the impulses we choose not to control,* and my aim has been to disarm myself, having realized that I've been like a ticking bomb all along by charging ahead with my life, instead of letting it unfold.

Putting my needs first when it came to interacting with my mother was like disobeying a direct order from my 'inner critic.' I didn't jump on a plane to see her before she died, having consulted with several friends and being told that I shouldn't go without a plan. Her heart condition was improving and she was due home in a few days, after which she'd require a live-in nurse as she dealt with her lung cancer. I declined to be that nurse, and didn't want to take the chance of needing to be hospitalized for depression in Romania. I'd heard enough about Romanian hospitals to worry me, and just said No. I turned off my phone for three days, and when I checked my email again at the library she was dead. I didn't go to be with my sister even then. An autopsy was done, then my mother was cremated. My sister took the ashes home to Switzerland with her. It was a bad ending to a long, difficult relationship.

I tried to continue working but bowed out of most of the work available to me. I shut myself in. I ended up on a psychiatric ward for five days. I'd wondered down the hallway of my building one early morning wrapped in only a blanket, paranoid. A neighbor called the police and they called an ambulance. One of the cops went in to my apartment for some clothes, and when the ambulance came I became belligerent so they cuffed me to a stretcher. I argued with the staff at the emergency room, until I got an injection of a powerful anti-psychotic and passed out.

When I was released it hadn't snowed yet, but it was cold. My roommate on the ward gave me a sweatshirt to put over what I was wearing. My parents' old neighbor had come to the hospital earlier that day to see me, and lent me twenty bucks to get some food at the 7Eleven next door. A cab paid for by the hospital brought me home. I didn't have my keys but the super let me in.

That manic episode for me was much like all the others I'd had, except in one way: I wasn't going back to my parents. The last time I'd been on a ward was thirteen years before, when both my parents were still alive. Two years before that I'd had a more extensive series of episodes, which let to my moving back from Brooklyn to my parents' house with only a few things and my sick cat. I lived with her in my parents' basement that spring, until she died.

As I look at this account of my life, it is confirmed that I reacted like a refugee all along. The apartment I lived in in Clark while I was helping to take care of my father, while I went to school for massage and later worked as a therapist, was a refuge. I thought I could have a cat because all my neighbors had pets, but it turned out that talking about it to the landlord was a mistake. I had gotten Josie as a kitten by 2002, but had to bring her to my parents' house, where she spent a lot of time hiding in the basement. I saw her every day, but it wasn't enough.

After my father died, I moved into the house of my new boyfriend in Cranford, just outrunning my mother again. With my boyfriend as a buffer, I had found shelter, finally, I thought. The feeling didn't last long, but some real distance was established between my mother and me as a result of my moving in. As her macular degeneration grew worse and she became unsafe to drive, I had to do what I'd never done, by standing up to her.

Eventually I went through the Department of Motor Vehicles to have her license taken away. I didn't realize how bad her vision really was until I sat in on an exam she had with a doctor who was filling in for her regular one. He came right out and told her she shouldn't be driving anymore. That came only days after I'd talked her into buying herself a new car which she promised to drive only on local streets and only during the day. She used that later on to say I'd tricked her into buying a new car that I wanted for myself. She called herself "my cash cow." My uncle in Romania refused to talk to me after that. She moved permanently back to Romania within a year, although my uncle had died in the interim. My aunt became her caregiver.

When I think of my relationship with my mother, I am hard-pressed to find anything positive about it. Did I take advantage of her, like she said, or was I just reacting to her prompts? Maybe something in between? What was going on between us was so much of a pattern that when her death ripped that fabric to shreds I was at a loss as to how to continue. I haven't forgiven myself yet, despite feeling that inclusive forgiveness is what needs to happen. What I do know is that very little of that relationship had to do with faith. I had functioned, but in the end my need to belong in my life in some way led back to mania, the only state in which I was completely self-confident.

Now, with the new medication this past year, with therapy and lately with the grief seminar and this job training class, faith in God has been reestablished. The more daunting task is to establish faith in myself, after so many years, practically my whole adult life. The last time I remember having complete faith in myself was before I left Romania to join my parents in the States, in '79. That's why I've gone back to it so much in my writing. I've needed to recreate some part of that original strength I had.

Moving away to Canada had helped too, in finding a calmer self. A couple of weeks ago I talked to my therapist about how I'd finally come to accept my failure then, after a series of hospitalizations in the spring of '94. My husband no longer wanted me, my parents didn't want me back, and the only reason I was still there into the summer was that I had to wait for a new passport, having thrown away my old one during a manic high. I can't tell exactly why, but I became resigned to my inability to change the situation. Then I became calm. That ironically made my husband want me again, so I stayed.

That is a pattern for me too, becoming calm and reacting well only when the playing field has been leveled. I just have to learn to do it without needing to go into a psychiatric ward for it. Last year, I made my way home in five days, while others had been there much longer. With the help that I'm getting, it may just be that I won't need that kind of intervention again.

When Dr. Low talked about preparing for *the inevitable setback,* he didn't mean just hospital stays, which is how I've looked at it. Preparing for minor setbacks is important too. Three years ago, I slipped back into a pattern of not consulting with a physician, and ultimately not taking medication other than what was available homeopathically. Dr. Low wouldn't have approved, but I had talked myself out of going to Recovery meetings by then too, which would have encouraged me to get help.

I was more of a refugee than ever, though I didn't see myself as one. I saw myself as functioning well in "the real world," dealing with regular problems, like regular people did. I talked myself into thinking I wasn't bipolar. It was important to have that image of myself to counter my mother's attitude toward me. If I had failed her, at least I was on my way to finally becoming successful financially. But somewhere along the way I began to slip into paranoia, and didn't see it. Old patterns came up again, of needing to have worth by imagining myself as crucial to the fate of the world. I had two lives, one in which I was a well-respected massage therapist, another in which it was alright to be as alone as I was, other than briefly indulging in physical needs.

Then, my mother was diagnosed with lung cancer, and there was the push to have me put my life on hold to come look after her. Any reason not to was seen as an excuse, although my sister lived closer. I felt I was being dragged into a potentially catastrophic situation, and put up as good as fight as I could, but it wasn't enough. With my mother's death, I'd failed more than ever. I was responsible for her death, I felt. With nothing left to defend, I crashed.

That brings me to now. Looking more carefully at my life through writing again has allowed me to see some of my strengths in a new light. And, for the first time, the pain I've felt for so many years is no longer denied. Like I did that summer in Alberta, I've finally had to accept a deep sense of failure. More time has passed, so the load is greater, but it's finally occurred to me that I can set it down. What I'm doing most of now, making my writing public again, is a form of healing, one that I couldn't ask anyone else to do for me. I can take my time now with what's made up my heavy load, deciding what needs to stay and what needs to go. It no longer feels like I have to get it all down before it disappears. Every day I face my anxiety, every day there are new challenges. Somehow, it is all more bearable.

P~art~ F~ive~

After several days of anxiety, I'm trying the trick of suspending disbelief again. It's been hard making it through a few hours, never mind a few days. Not showing up for class Thursday or Friday brought me to a new threshold: I was convinced that I wouldn't be allowed back. I felt that I was proving I can't stick it out, again, this time because of the weather. The snow storm was a week ago.

I thought I wouldn't be able to do anything but retreat into my corner. Now something has given way; I am more at ease, boiling potatoes to mash and watching a comedy. I did laundry this morning and then went to the bank to close my business account, which I've been meaning to do. Doing it brought to mind that I really won't be doing massage for a living anymore, that it's not just something that might or might not happen. That brought on anxiety, but after a good adventure movie I was distracted from my worrying enough to witness a shift for the better as it happened.

I've needed to feel a part of things, to have a purpose. This week, with class canceled Tuesday and Wednesday, I did some more writing. Every time I've come to the end of a chapter it's been very much an act of 'daring to exist.' With this last one, anxiety came up so strong that I canceled the taxi for the next morning to go to class. Then I left a message for the director of the program to let her know that I was experiencing high anxiety and wouldn't be able to make it in. Making my apologies, I felt like a complete failure again.

On Monday I'd driven into Elizabeth for a session with my therapist and hadn't found a parking spot. Calling in to the program two days later, I felt helpless. I had a strong sense of imminent danger, even with all my Recovery training. The snow was so high in the streets through Wednesday that I felt trapped.

This makes me realize that some of my anxiety in March and April of last year was a compounded state of helplessness not unlike this one, just deeper. What got me out of that one was intense meditative prayer, so I've been trying that again since yesterday. Something has shifted.

The program director called me yesterday to ask me not to give up on the class or on myself. She offered to go out of her way next Tuesday, if necessary, to help me find a parking spot. It might be that it's not even about parking or taking a taxi or a bus to get there. It's at least in part about the writing. That is something that my mother would disapprove of; any time I've affirmed myself in this way it's been as if I've stood up to strong gusts of wind and been pushed right down by them.

Fear used to be about being found out as a mistake, an impostor, something else than what I was putting across at first sight. Even with my history of hospitalizations, I was only posing as mentally ill, I thought, being sure that it couldn't really be true. I needed to write, to find a way not to be bipolar, as if it were something I could talk myself out of. I wrote about being bipolar as a way of distancing myself from it. Now it's about becoming a source of insight which might be useful to others. I can't live my life always wanting something and then running away from it when it's finally in sight. After all this writing, it's scary that someone might actually read it, but I have to take a chance on it anyway.

Finding a purpose is still about seeking worth. I still haven't forgiven myself, I still need redemption. What was debilitating this week will turn out, in the future, to be just a bump in the road, as a friend referred to my severe depression last year. She was right. I did recover. I was even able to hold on to most of the ground I'd gained as I went, which was new. Today I can hope that after as powerful a wave of discomfort as I've experienced this week, I'll be able to hold on to the reprieve that has been granted. This morning I was ready to move through another day of anxiety the best I could. Now something has given way. Same apartment, same everything, but something has budged.

There is a part of me which is so hurt that it can do nothing but anticipate disaster, doom, and failure, a part which is stuck in warning mode. The process goes back to being twelve-years-old and feeling hurt by my father's lack of trust. I felt betrayed, though I couldn't identify that feeling at the time. Later, when I did, it got buried in guilt. I would have wanted him to trust me enough to tell me that he and my mother weren't coming back from their trip to the West. It was impractical for many reasons to have him do that, but I still would have wanted him to trust me that much; up to that time I had done the same for him. I thought I knew my father, but it turned out that I didn't.

Both my parents worked very hard; I never got to know either of them in Romania. My sister and I had a nanny. I also had my grandmother, who took me to the eye clinic in the capital where she lived, as often as possible, to work on correcting my crossed eyes. By the time I was eleven they were straight, and I'd had much-needed nurturing from her.

In the United States my family entered a routine that was very different from what I'd known; Nonna was no longer the head of the family, my mother was. Now, so much later, I am trying to undo damage going back that far, though it becomes clear that what I need to do even more is to accept myself as I was at the time. Like the kid in the old soup commercial, who'd turned into a snowman, my young self must be allowed into a warm kitchen to thaw out and enjoy the nourishment provided. The self that I am now must see to the needs of my self then.

The more it happens, the more I, as I am now, realize how much damage was done to the girl I was then. Every time anyone comes near, she has trouble distinguishing between good and bad. The alarm sounds either way and she runs and hides. Punishment is expected, and she does her best to guard against it, through isolation. It was in this context that terror struck again, when I finished my latest little bit of writing.

Although my mother had been dead for over a year, my younger self knew only the pattern of getting punished for standing up to her. She'd paid attention when my mother had said that my writing could give her a heart attack or a stroke. It shouldn't have been an issue anymore, but there it was, still. To the question "What would your mother say?" the 'inner critic', always present, would find an answer that would make my young self responsible for imaginary harm done. If I dared to exist by publishing my writing yet again, it threatened, my young self would be the one to feel the heat. This time I felt the effects of the alarm loud and clear, not like in the past when I was writing to prove something, and discomfort was a price worth paying. Now I see the amount of harm my 'inner critic' is capable of.

The self that I am now experiences the chemical aspect of anxiety, which renders me unable to function. I am grateful, though, for the insight this last stretch of anxiety has brought me: that part of me, the survivor part, is still alive and not to be destroyed. Nonna's love allows for its survival. With love and encouragement, it may come out more, in time.

But it may be a long time yet, because the twelve-year-old in me can't tell the difference in touch between the old and the new. She's weary of interaction because of the many times touch has been deceptive. My 'inner critic' is guarding her fiercely, being aware that it might just be within reach for that same kid to finally join what could become a complete human being. She has been looking for a place to belong, a home, as have I. We are one and the same in our weariness of the world around us, having incurred similar damage. If we manage to reach each other and communicate our love for each other, the 'inner critic' might just lose the war.

Thus, my life now does have a purpose: integrating the parts left behind. Even the critic, now so busy threatening utter collapse, once had a positive role of helping guard against excesses. It too must be allowed to heal. There are no more enemies, there is no one who is entirely at fault at the expense of others. What matters is that now, in the present moment, a truce can be sought. For the enemy factions to come together to the bargaining table, I have to do more of the same: show up in my life if I can, excuse myself if I can't, retreat from it if I feel overwhelmed.

The damaged part of my self exists only in spirit, now, but has been denied love even in that respect for much too long. I have grown into a woman, but without the child that I was I can't fully be myself. What I would like to get across to her is that I know I can't have *temper at the illness,* finally, and that *not having the luxury of temper* is okay. She needs to know that I won't be engaging our 'inner critic' in any more battles, having understood that when I do, it is she who gets punished. She knows how to hide, but only for so long: she always gets found out in the end.

Writing confuses the 'inner critic,' it turns out. Negative core beliefs, when forced into a new course away from vital functions, create strong feelings of anxiety and pain, but have to comply eventually. *Symptoms lose their validity with daily contradiction.* Doing two difficult things at once, such as publishing again and establishing a new pattern in the same day, has proved debilitating this week. Taking a leap of faith brought pain, like the first time, twenty-six years ago, and all the times in between. Only here I am still, writing about it. That matters.

It is by writing without rancor that the freedom of my younger self will be won. She is still nervous about it, but is grateful to see that I am willing to put myself in the way of force that used to be daunting, and survive the event. She might just trust me enough to bring up other challenges over time, finding that she will no longer have to face them alone. Our home is our refuge; the cats, with their calming presence, are part of the whole; the bills are paid; a new beginning is made. Neglected parts can be reconsidered.

I am able to physically go outside and accomplish tasks as they present themselves, like going to see my therapist tomorrow and going food shopping later. Nervous though I am, I will *anticipate joyfully or not at all.* I will take what precautions I can and carry my cell phone in case of need. Despite experiencing nerve endings which are still raw from similar challenges last week, I will dare to go out there, and function. When it comes to this, I have less courage than my younger self, but she might lend me hers now and then as I go, in fact she's already intervened through Nonna's presence. What gives me courage is that we will face things together.

Through the process of recovery which is at work, I glimpsed last night what I may be allowed to feel more of: the feeling of belonging in my own life. Without being manic, having relied only on several light movies, I got a sense of belonging. That is important, because my younger self allowed herself to be noticed on a quiet day. Normally she is a fierce warrior, but this time ease was the topic of the day, and she was able to partake. She still felt like a foreigner, but a little less so by the end of the day. I noticed her presence because I finally stopped and looked. We met half-way. Now I'm more grateful than ever for the American way, which has allowed for this much.

Over a year ago, I shifted my pattern away from jumping to rescue my mother, and ended up in a collapse. I can see that now as what needed to happen. My initial leap into mania so many years ago was similar, so I can work on healing that old wound as I heal the most recent one. Something was wrong then, something I couldn't bear, or even define. Now I am in an environment that allows for rebuilding. I just have to take things one at a time, dismantling what I can of the 'inner critic' in a non-combative way. Piece of cake. It's important to know that it's the strength of the little girl I was, that has allowed for it. Just as I kept all of my essential files inside Anne's old computer, then brought them out a little at a time, I kept that essential young part of me alive, deep inside. She is of the Old World, I am of the New, but for me to function, both parts must come together.

That is why I experienced so much anxiety last Wednesday night. I directly disobeyed my 'inner critic' by leaving yet another trace on a potentially large canvas, through writing. I've made it increasingly hard for 'negative core beliefs' to rub out that part of my life. By publishing yet another chapter, I took a chance and dared to exist again, like I'd done at twenty-two, in art school. This time, without my parents standing by, I didn't have anyone to flesh out the danger I felt, but the punishment came swiftly enough anyway. That fit right in with the old pattern, of expecting punishment for having chosen to look out for myself instead of for my mother.

I come out of the experience with two things, today: one, that in time I will heal by not being separate from my younger self anymore, and two, that I can begin to negotiate my complete freedom as a human being by showing a healthy respect for the power an 'inner critic' can have. Three days ago I knew only that I'd failed again, completely this time, because I'd had too much anxiety about going to class. A day later I was treated with compassion and understanding by the class director, which also left me feeling raw because it seemed to me I didn't deserve it. Yesterday I stopped everything, prayed and meditated, and gave myself only the challenge of lightening my own load by watching light movies and taking their message only at face value.

I thought a lot about the time in Canada in '94 when I was able to accept myself as beaten by events I couldn't control, and had become calm again as a result. This morning I have been made aware, through more prayer and meditation, that there is a young part of me which I've neglected, but which has hung in there and will reclaim her full role in my life, if only I allow it.

At twelve, I hadn't "accomplished" or "achieved" anything yet. I was still just a kid. It was after coming to the United States to join my parents that the burden of achievement was placed on me. With that, I lost my sense of humor and did my best to comply. With that, my 'inner critic' took shape. It ate up anything I accomplished as I grew older, always dissatisfied. It embedded in me the sense of never being enough, of being doomed to fail, so that any achievement would be discounted almost upon completion. My graduation from art school was like that. Any value it had was deeply overshadowed by the defeat, strongly felt in the family, of my bipolar diagnosis.

In this light, I can see my current physical weakness as positive, having allowed for so much introspection. I have simplified my life and acknowledged my limitations. The process of my recovery has not come to a dead stop as a result, like it felt on Thursday. I knew only raw nerves that day, but I functioned, went to the library, put in an application to a temp agency, then went shopping. My sense of failure that night was complete: I was the impostor again. How could I work, I was telling myself, if I couldn't even show up for class. My 'negative core beliefs' were potent, my 'inner critic' was winning. But I made it through.

On the morning of my birthday my symptoms were still strong, even after the class director called and reassured me that I would have a second chance. My crisis had been real, and my nervous anticipation lasted for days, but something has shifted with the new awareness of myself, as fractioned and yet capable of becoming coherent again. I prayed for help this morning, and it has been granted. Time to eat something healthy and move on to the rest of the day. I may doubt every action at intervals, but I will know better than to provoke my 'inner critic' through temper again, as the day goes on.

Writing is an affirmation rather than a provocation. That process is taking its course too. I've been able to shift in this essential way. I can now conceive of "not speaking ill of the dead," in the future. A deliberate shift in this direction will allow for change. It needs to happen, since it is what will ensure the release of my younger self. Once she can go replenish herself fully, she will come stand with me again, but not before. In the meantime, my frazzled nerves will deal with more anxiety, but the intensity associated with the process will diminish.

Today was the graduation ceremony for my course. I made it. This morning I was so anxious about it that I treated myself to one last cab ride, to and from Elizabeth. I was concerned about parking again, being that it was Thursday and there would be limited spots, due to street cleaning rules. My sense of inadequacy as a result was intense, but it was more important not to worry about potential damage to my car, or about having it towed, than to spare myself the expense.

I don't have a job yet, but I am taking steps which I've skipped, as far back as my early twenties. That is my accomplishment for today; luckily my sense of failure was held in check because I realized that much. It was enough that everyone was sincerely at ease, that we'd made it through the six weeks together.

In Recovery they say to *bear the discomfort and comfort will come.* As uncomfortable as I've been at times through this process, it was very important to finish what I'd started. This morning it was very important to own my life until now, complete with feelings of inadequacy. I have done a lot of damage, I thought, and I can't take any of it back, but I can influence what comes next.

There are no uncontrollable impulses, only the impulses we choose not to control. I had planned ahead to get in my car when I got home and go food shopping without coming in first, and I was able to do that. Doing what I'd planned was important. This morning I was *in duality,* and when we're in duality we must *plan, decide and act,* which I did. When I did get home after shopping I *endorsed* myself, because *when we're endorsing ourselves we're not blaming ourselves.* I'm more grateful than ever for the fact that so much of my Recovery training has stayed with me.

Two factors are at work now, as I get my footing in a new stage of my life: making attempts to improve my state through *will training,* and allowing for more and more faith to come in. One of the volunteer teachers present this morning mentioned that trusting in God's will is as important as believing in Him. I had said that there is a clear willingness to help the needy of so many kinds, among people of faith, more so than within the general population.

When I was at Cooper I was trying to establish for myself the worth of artistic pursuit as a manifestation of my devotion to God. I pushed too hard and collapsed. What I'm doing now is picking up the pieces as if the crisis had just happened. At the time I couldn't do as much. Now there is no one left to blame, there is no one coercing me into behavior that they see as fitting. My addiction to dependent behavior is clearly my challenge. My bipolar diagnosis from back then is no longer the issue. There will be no magic wand to sweep me into a form of success which could "show them all."

What is painful is the realization that my initial collapse wasn't a fateful punishment for trying to acknowledge my faith in God. It was part of a long process by which my faith in God has been reaffirmed. I was never abandoned. I had tried to stand by my family, hoping they would help me up when I fell, not realizing that they were incapable of the kind of support I needed. Now, so much later, I can forgive them and myself for trying too hard. With time passing after my mother's death, I am finally able to grieve my own losses as well as my parents', with renewed faith in God, Nonna, and The Way.

It has gotten very cold out. I will not go outside today. Plans to spend some time with a new friend have also been suspended, for the same reason. As it was, I could feel anxiety settling in this morning, and I was honest about it when she called to cancel. Now the question is, how to approach the rest of the day.

My anxiety has tapered a little, in the early afternoon. I just watched a movie. The cats are sleeping peacefully in their favorite places. I hear the wind blowing outside and am grateful for this apartment, for my home. The apartment we lived in as a family fresh from Romania was rented too. Within a couple of years my parents bought the house on Locust Drive; I am still here after almost five years. They made something happen which I haven't been able to do.

Can I forgive myself for being too good for some and not good enough for others? This is what gets me stuck. It goes all the way back to being twelve and having my life change so much, so fast. The smart, funny kid that I was must be allowed in, if I am to heal and function. She knows the right time to try for a positive leap more than I do.

Writing helps me refer to other rites of passage, giving me hope that in time I will make it past this tide. In this same apartment I have matured and come to accept my limitations. Today I have that mild head pressure which has been present whenever I face 'negative core beliefs.' I must let it all pass without trying to win.

I've done a lot of that: I've tried to figure out how to win over my 'inner critic,' not realizing that there would be no end to it. My young self was held back by this same critic, that was all I knew. I wanted justice for her. She was unable to communicate with me directly, and every time she tried to she was thrown back. But she kept trying, and now the distance has been breached. That gives me hope.

Having things seems pointless if I am not allowed to function as a complete human being. In the past I've tried to put other people in the role of the one who might complete my life for me. First I took care of my father, the best I could, until I started growing into a woman and he took interest in me in an inappropriate way. Then my mother wanted me to fill the role of confidant after my grandmother died. I couldn't do that because I didn't trust her, but she persisted, feeling so alone in her life with my father. Like various people since, my parents saw uses for me, and insisted that I comply.

The malaise that is manifesting again today is related to not coming through for my parents, for my mother especially. I hadn't realized before my mother's death that I'd held on so much to my former role in her life, of caregiver, even from far away. In the end I failed her when she needed me most, when she was dying. I had to choose between her needs and mine, and I chose mine.

On a day like today I need to 'check the facts' again. Last year at this time I was still coming down off a manic high. I am more grateful than I can say for the fact that it was caught early; over the past year my chemistry has been balanced to the point of my functioning and taking distance from events in my life, in ways I haven't before. The help that I'm getting confronts behavior that has been in place for thirty-six years, which brings on more malaise, like going through withdrawal cold-turkey. There is no other way, though. Getting something down on paper most days will have to do, until there is less of what stops me from functioning.

Am I really alone? The answer is no. There's the 'inner critic,' ready to have me give up on myself some more. But there are also positive influences, and that young kid that I was. I will make it to the next day, and the next. The more important thing is to take all the blows that come myself, instead of letting my younger self try to take them, anymore. We aren't entirely disconnected now, which means she can tell me when I need to step in, and I'm glad to do it. She's been the source of hope that's kept me going all these years, I just didn't know it because I hadn't been able to take any distance from the situation. It's time to see this as a tag team effort, in which she can comment but no longer has to take the blows.

Something happened about the time Nonna died: I left my younger self behind. Life became about proving something, more so than it had been before. The sense of loss after each failure was pushed into the background. As I write today, seeing it as part of the process of recovery, I feel mostly defeat. I made it through the job skills class but still have no job. I'm still hard on myself. But I know that I'll make it through the day, because I make it through every day. There is no set date for a positive shift but I know from experience that it will come when it needs to.

So how have I failed so completely, and whom? When did it start, and how did it manifest? I know the answers, but don't dare bring them up. My depression is centered around not feeling that I have the right to speak up. Like in the basic acting classes when I was an "extra," my voice trembles and I can't get the words out. Or like fifteen years ago when I joined the church choir and nearly fainted the first time we would all sing together in front of the whole congregation. I bowed out of both, much like I'm bowing out of social interaction now. I know that no one else can do it for me, I know that the effort can be made, but I choke anyway. Then I feel that my family were right, back in '89, to tell me that no one will want me anymore. They saw me as a liability after that, and I became one. Now, there is no one left to defy, but there were no plans made for my surviving beyond this point, either.

Still, here I am. In a day or two I will reread my notes and will be able to draw something from them. For now, there is only the feeling of pulling teeth just to get through the day. But I'm glad to do it, because withdrawal for me means withdrawal for the kid that I was, too. There's no other way to get through it, at least none that I can think of. I am grateful that all the basics are covered, all the bills are paid, and all I have to do is get through the heaviness.

Then a little clarity comes through: I have been making an impossible comparison. I am comparing my accomplishments to my parents'. No wonder I always fall short. How could I, at twelve, and as the fractured self I've been since then, compare myself to my parents? They made it through very difficult events as they were growing up, and then had relative success when they picked themselves up and took such a chance on coming to the U.S. I was supposed to take the baton and run with it when my time came, but I couldn't. I stumbled and fell, and became a disappointment.

And yet what people see is someone who made it through a good art school, who picked herself up and functioned more than once, who is worth the trouble of helping. Instinctively I ask for help, and when it comes I fill in as much as I can of the next step, then collapse again. It happened this last time too, with the snowstorm halfway through the six-week course.

The routine I'd settled into was fractured, and I remained in panic mode even though I was able to return and finish the class. Here I am, dealing with what's left of the anxiety. My young self whispers that I should leave her behind and save myself. She doesn't understand yet that we are not separate anymore. It is up to me to let her know that between us she is the wise and funny one, the one to be nurtured, before anything else can take place.

With that, I will break and make lunch. At Cooper, we took turns forging ahead and forgot to eat, forgot to sleep, forgot to laugh. We both leapt into the unknown. It was with that first fall that we lost our connection, until this past year. Lunch it is, then, later a nap with the cats, then maybe a movie or two. It is alright to take the time to heal.

This much comes through clearly: my leap was different from my parents', but I was trying for the same thing: success. I wanted their dreams of me to come true. They had succeeded. I wanted them to be proud of my success too; I wanted to be loved and accepted as an artist. They saw the artist in me as the cause of my collapse, of their shame; things went from there. I had tried for a connection with God while becoming an artist, and there I lost them, because they didn't have a connection with God themselves. After that, they did their best to correct my behavior, but failed.

Another day brings with it the certainty that I will get through as many days as I need to. It no longer feels like I will never belong in my life. Today, writing turns out to be a choice, not a necessity. Trusting in God can come along with believing in God. In that light, I feel there is a purpose to my being here. It is important to remember that I've had low self-esteem for a long time, and that changing that will take time. Today I have a little more distance again.

Healing comes in waves too, not only pain. As ocean waves pull back, they leave the beach changed, though many waves must pass before the change is evident. My old self wants change to come fast, afraid of losing the little bit that was gained. The self I am now must hold her own for a while longer, before there can be proof of a definable shift.

When I'm low on supplies I panic a little, no matter what it is I'm running out of. I panic a little and then go over a way to fix it. Right now I'm low on certainty. What that shows me, when I take the time and distance to consider it, is that a change is coming. I can't be certain of anything in the middle of a change, other than staying open. It feels today like my young self, who's been so frightened for so long, is beginning to trust again too.

As long as we stick to the budget, there will be plenty of time to unwind to a healthy state, so that "the inside will match the outside." I don't want to scare anyone anymore, but I don't want to hide my history of mental illness either. There will be a balance, in time. I keep thinking that I have to figure it out on my own and act according to a set plan, but it turns out that I don't. Help is there as soon as I allow for it. When there's been enough withdrawal, my chemistry will shift on its own. I don't have to know when, I just have to trust that it will.

With focus being so much on myself, during my isolation, the rooms of my home have felt bare, in the bright light of day. I have counted my defects and not seen my qualities. Today I chose a pink shirt to wear. Colors make a difference.

Tomorrow it may snow again. This might turn into a long weekend. Today is Valentine's Day, and beautiful out. I watched a favorite movie, I made lunch and savored it, I took a nap with Vinny and played with The Kiddo, I ironed what I didn't get to, last night.

I have been feeling like someone wanted to push me out of my own life again, up to today. But I didn't budge. Today is a good day to look over the past year and count all my accomplishments as a way of reminding myself that a job is not the only way to feel worthy. Writing has helped.

There was a point, a couple of years ago, when I owned only two work shirts and two sets of slacks. I was eating brown rice and trout stuffed with crab meat, apples, and not much more. I was taking only "Happy Camper" and finding my self-worth completely dependent on how good a job I did with each massage. I didn't realize that I was slipping into paranoia.

I had adopted Mr.Greulich's cat and we were getting along. Mr.Greulich hadn't been diagnosed with cancer yet, neither had my mother.

My sense of purpose now is different than it was then. I didn't realize how precarious my situation was, at the time. I was mostly aware of the game my mother and I used to play with each other. I wonder what she thinks of me now. Maybe she doesn't think of me anymore, or maybe she is angrier with me than ever. Either way, I have to let her go.

I think of my staples. It was hard, losing access to the one store I shopped at in Westfield. They had the best brown rice since I can remember. The parking at my regular supermarket has gotten so difficult that I've stopped going there. That is a lot to get used to in a short time. It means that I have to take the time to adjust my pattern, which has been to shop every couple of days, also for the purpose of seeing familiar faces. I have enough of everything to get through another snow storm if need be, tomorrow, but by the following day I will have to go shopping.

I wonder now how it was that I got so anxious driving into Elizabeth after the last snow storm. What about it set me off, exactly. The obvious reason is that the streets weren't cleared for days, but was there more than that? I was very afraid of damage being done to my car. I feel some anxiety now just thinking about it. Maybe I was right to be concerned.

I would like to think that I don't have to edit myself so much. That makes me think that maybe I should look for work in places where I won't have to hide my mental illness. I don't want to have people scared of me anymore. Doing massage, I got very good at passing for normal. I was good enough at it not to have to explain my life, and mostly I didn't share being bipolar. Now I don't want to hide who I am anymore.

Is there something wrong with me because I'm a manic depressive? If the answer that pops up in your mind is "obviously!", you're thinking much like I have, all these years. The trick is to take a chemical imbalance at face value, instead of continuing to assume the worst about the person who has it, especially if that person is you, but even if it isn't. I know how to withdraw from various settings "before it shows," but I don't want to live like that anymore.

There are people who have come to accept me as I am. Soon, I hope to be one of them. Having a mental illness has outweighed all positive aspects of my life for a long time. I've hidden for far too long. Now I have to gingerly lead my young, frightened self into the light at a rate she can handle. There's a budget for it, so it can finally happen.

Knowing that much allows for purpose during an unplanned day. Not pushing is key. A sense of anxiety is to be expected, and often comes. Patience is very important. What that allows for is pulling out strands of what used to cause terror, one by one, as a means of showing myself that all discomfort can be borne.

So when the thought of running low on printer ink shoots through me, I need to tell myself that I didn't get a backup on purpose. That I wanted to deal with that kind of anxiety only when the time came, not before. Like with the rice from my favorite store, I have to trust that I will be able to get some of comparable quality and value at whatever store I look for rice in next. When I'm running low on orange juice and mineral water, I have to remind myself that I've gotten through on filtered water for years. When I realize that it's time to buy a new filter, I need to put it on the list and only get more than one if there's a good sale. It goes on like that.

Being that it's Valentine's Day, I am aware of not having a boyfriend, but I don't have a sinking feeling about it today, as I've had in the past. I need him, when he does enter my life, not to be even remotely scared of my being bipolar. I no longer have the energy to explain my illness. It has to be alright that I'm doing everything that I can to live with it fully, not in a fragmented way. If that's not enough, I will have to pass, until it is.

The change is part of the process of acceptance too, of my own self. My mother used to say I should use my looks to "get" some unsuspecting guy before he realizes I'm bipolar. Having her reinforce that over time didn't help. She only wanted the best for me, but it came out wrong. I've made a habit of not letting anyone close because I didn't want to have the kind of success that is based on a lie.

Other than that, I am giving myself a break from job-searching until the next time I make it to the library. The listings online seem haphazard to me. I need to simmer down and hopefully be inspired, as I have been in the past, to try for a new approach at the right time. The essential thing is not to be desperate. I have taken great pains not to seem desperate, but it's even more important to really not be desperate. For a year, I've approached working as the one thing that would give me value, and when I hurt my knee last September the sense of failure was complete: I had to give up massage too. It's for the best, but it's created a lot of anxiety. As the need for that anxiety fades, as I become more confident, I am more likely to feel that I belong in my life, fully, for the first time.

The thing is to *drop the judgement,* to stop knocking my head against the wall when I find myself needing to start over. I have a lot to start over with. I just need to know that, through and through. Just as there's a budget for groceries and household expenses, there needs to be an internal budget for building self-confidence, mostly time and the willingness to reassure the part of me which is scared; to go through withdrawal; to allow the part that got so used to being needy, emotionally and financially, to unwind. Being needy was what was asked of me by my mother, and it's how I've lived.

Seeing Tootsie again brought to mind, as it always does, the memory of Tom kissing me for the first time. We had just seen *Tootsie* together at the Roselle Park theater, back when I was sixteen. It was my first kiss. I bit his tongue, I remember. We were double-dating with my sister and Richard, and my sister turned around suddenly to say something, in the car. Tom and I were in the back seat. I remember all his kisses as one event now, as one of the happiest memories of my life. I wasn't ready for more than that, so we didn't, but I was very much in love. My mother drove him away, but before she did he left a permanent mark.

Every time I see this movie I think of Tom and how close we got. Tonight especially, it being Valentine's Day, the thought of him grounded me more than I thought it might, because it occurred to me that I was bipolar from birth, and that Tom cared for me despite my being a manic depressive. He loved our kisses as much as I did, and he loved my long hair, asked me to never cut it. Life was much simpler then. The day Nonna came to the camp I worked in, the following summer, she brought me a letter that had come for me at the house. It was from Tom. It was scented, I remember. Sending me that letter was the sweetest thing anyone had ever done for me. Nonna died two weeks later, and Tom was there for me at the funeral.

Something good happened tonight: I realized that I was bipolar from birth. That's important, because here I am in Roselle Park, two streets in from Cranford, and I found the "reset" point that I've been looking for. That memory made me remember that I was always very sensitive, which for me is part of being bipolar, but that back when I was sixteen that was a good thing. It was what drew Tom to me and me to him.

Bipolar disorder is something that is passed on genetically, it's not something learned or fallen into. Addictions can come with it, depending on circumstances, but the illness itself is not something that I could have helped; in high school, and then in college, my sensitivity was only one part of me, maybe an underlying part, but not all there was. I was also smart and funny and someone nice to have around. I am still that person. I just have to remember that. So here I am, being with my two cats in my home tonight, feeling part of something. Thank you, Nonna.

Some turning points we see coming, others we only become aware of afterwards. I am trying for something in between. I have been dependent for so long. I think now that I never fully expected to make it financially as a massage therapist. I got paid, but for something which came as a gift. I felt bad taking money for it. What it comes down to is that I didn't feel like I deserved to get paid, no matter what job I had. I couldn't fully see myself in any of the jobs I had, as if I was just waiting around to be terminated by a higher power.

It only becomes obvious now that I was waiting for what happened last year, with my mother's death. I was totally thrown off course. I had known only to survive, and when the war finally ended I was left holding the bag of my old patterns. They were so entrenched that I couldn't put them down, I couldn't start over. And, I had to finally own being bipolar, given the episode I had.

Checking the facts again, I see that I am dressed, I've functioned, tonight I will take an Epsom salt bath and prepare for tomorrow. If the snow comes (just saying it brings a wave of anxiety,) I will postpone my meeting with my therapist. My cats are at ease, I am doing much better than yesterday. Less of the weight of the world has settled on my shoulders today. There has to be someone out there who will see me as a worthy mate, someday. To him, I send a Valentine in advance. No more need to run, no more need to catch up with what others are doing in their own life. Writing does it, for now.

Having been told recently by a relative stranger that most people would run the other way once they'd heard I'm bipolar, I am left to wonder tonight if I really scared my parents, as my mother told me I did. It never occurred to me to run away from her because of her depression, but manic depression registers differently. I don't think I ever believed that my mother was, or could be, afraid of me. I was a constant adversary and a burden to her, but I really think I was much more afraid of her than she was of me.

In the family, I learned to attack when cornered. My parents had been defending themselves and their turf for a long time, since their teens. They had the refugee approach, as I thought of it. I think what happened was that they took for granted that I was on their side and I took for granted that, despite our differences, they were on my side. With such high expectations it's not a surprise, in retrospect, that my being diagnosed as bipolar brought as much disappointment as it did, to all involved.

After it happened, they needed to hide me away. I am thinking of this without judgement, tonight. It has taken a very long time to get to feeling this way about it, but now that I can say it in earnest it helps me a lot, in letting go. Maybe I can come out of the shadows of my own life as a result.

Knowing myself well enough to be able to weigh the pluses and minuses, I must say that it surprised me this past week to hear I could scare anyone. But then, it's not unusual for people to fear what they don't understand. Maybe that's all that happened: a big misunderstanding as to what I could help and what I couldn't, and why, and what to do about it.

Maybe my family just wanted me to stop being mad at them. I pushed, they got defensive. They had more force, I caved in. That was supposed to be that. But it wasn't. For twenty-five years, I tried to win my way back to that first judgement of defeat, so that maybe I could change the outcome. It was the underlying theme to everything I did. I tried to turn the clock back to a time when I might have had a chance at not being a failure. Even when I thought I'd walked away from the struggle, I hadn't. That only became evident when my mother died.

As I thought, insight comes in waves. I return to old topics cyclically, as if sifting with a finer and finer sieve every time. It's important to know when to walk away, or to set things aside for a while. I return tonight to that comment, that most people would run the other way if they found out I'm bipolar. Considering how I've been able to make people feel comfortable for years, it seems strange to consider the possibility of frightening anyone. But I did, last year, enough so that the police were called, in the early morning when I was hospitalized.

I probably frightened my family in the same way, because I wasn't making sense and would stop listening to reason periodically. That I can understand. But most of the time, when I've been on medication, there's been no issue at all. Why would anyone feel the need to run away from me while I'm making as much sense as they do. Was the potential of another manic episode strong enough to scare my family, and would it be enough among the general population? I got tangled up in the web of what I needed to have happen with those close to me.

Another comment from years ago comes to mind: that people who are diagnosed with bipolar disorder "never make it back." If that were true, that would account for the fear strong enough to run the other way. But I have made it back, in fact I never left. I just got stuck trying to solve a problem that had no solution: I tried to make my family love me. No one can do that. They either do or they don't. Love can't be forced. But I can see now how it would be hard for an outsider to not want to run when the perception is that once diagnosed as bipolar the only thing to expect is more episodes. What has helped me lately is realizing that I don't want to "make it back" anymore, because that place of origin no longer exists. There're no more parents to convince that it's okay to love me anyway, despite my "faults."

And here it comes back to what I've been thinking about: manic depression isn't a "fault," mine or my parents'. I inherited genetic traits from them, they inherited genetic traits from their parents or grandparents, etc. What made things so difficult was the need to find out who did what wrong. I didn't want people to feel sorry for me, but that's what happened, enough so that I became accustomed to it, like a habit. I'm making efforts now to let go of that behavior, gradually, so that the addiction will become manageable as for anyone in recovery. In the job skills class it felt alright to mention being bipolar to the teachers as an explanation of all the holes in my resume. I was only feeling sorry for myself halfway. I was reaching for acceptance, and mostly I found it. The question that kept coming up was, when will you get on with your life?

Maybe the answer to that is Now because, other than not working yet, I am dealing with concerns that were never dealt with before. Not being desperate and not behaving like a refugee needed to happen before I could move forward. In this light, it's extremely good that I'm taking time to heal. That way, when the time comes, I will be able to really contribute something to my environment, not just pretend to do it, all the while exhausting my inner resources. All the pretending has worn me down at intervals. There would be no point to entering a job feeling like that. I need it to be alright to be me. In time, the grief of not hearing that from my parents will fade, and I will move on to a more productive part of my life. For the moment, I need to stay with the effort to heal.

A new batch of short grain brown rice is cooking on the stove. I got it yesterday from a store I hadn't shopped in before. Outside it's gray and cool, after all the warm rain yesterday. Most of the snow is gone. Yesterday, by mistake, I opened an old picture file of the bedroom in my apartment. It brought me back. I had deleted all my old pictures of it but there was a folder of pictures of my old cat Josie and some of them were also of the apartment; there was even one of the old apartment in Clark. The question came to mind right away: would I have done anything differently? The answer came easily: No. That's because even when I can't grasp at any sense of purpose, I know it is there.

It has taken a long time, but this morning it was very clear that I no longer function out of anger; it has sunk in that I *can't afford the luxury of temper.* Last night and this morning I went over all the class notes for the Word program. A couple of hours ago, when I was done, I felt intimidated again by what it may take to find a job. I ate lunch and gave myself a break, lying down with Vinny. I looked at *secure thought* after *secure thought,* and it worked. I reminded myself of all the progress I've made in the past year. I meditated, I prayed.

Now Vinny is napping in his favorite chair next to me, The Kiddo is resting under the couch. Here comes a wave of anxiety. Time to *trigger-spot. It's not how you feel it's how you function; humor is our best friend, temper is our worst enemy; symptoms rise and fall and run their course if we don't attach danger to them; I can substitute secure thoughts for insecure thoughts, be occupied rather than preoccupied; the resoluteness of the muscles will overcome the defeatism of the brain, and it's okay to do motionless sitting; feelings are not facts – they lie and deceive us and tell us of dangers that are not there.*

I keep thinking of how I've scared people in the past. It's true that *angry temper* is energizing for short bursts before exhaustion sets in. There is a connection there to patterns related to negative core beliefs. I learned intimidation a little too well in the family, growing up. Now there's no more room for that. I need to *drop the judgement* against myself and others.

Establishing healthy new patterns goes directly against the stream of my 'negative core beliefs,' or what makes up my 'inner critic.' Yesterday I functioned well, accomplishing all the things I had set out to do. By late afternoon I had even sent off a resume for another job, this time something close by, that I felt I'd be good at. I haven't heard back, a day later, but doing it felt great.

On the one hand, I can see positive changes as they're happening. On the other, I am aware of all the old destructive behavior of the past, and am daunted by how much unlearning I still need to do. One very secure thought is that I have time to go through the process. I have a budget to go on, which will allow for it.

Years ago I used to be afraid of getting angry, because that led to intense depression and ultimately to mania, even with medication. My mother and I were in such a *temperamental deadlock* that I often fell into anger, no matter how much I tried to avoid it. I was always on the defensive. What came down with such a loud thud, when she died, was that I'd spent my entire adult life learning damaging habits, each of which would have to be unlearned in time.

I have sought approval from various people I've looked up to. Acceptance from them would lead, at least for a little while, to a more balanced state. I would pile up happy moments as barricades for when the time came to talk to my mother again. I was still in that pattern this past year, after her death, aiming to downplay the comments of my 'inner critic,' who was always there to tell me that, "if they only knew", "they" wouldn't want me around.

As far as mentioning that I'm bipolar, I was told more gently not to do it right away, at different times. In Recovery, the *spotting* is *we don't need outer approval, we only need our own inner approval. Secure thoughts* tie into that.

A change that has already come, thankfully, is that I no longer think of myself as of someone I too would run away from, if I could. In the past few months *secure thoughts* as to my character have come up more steadily, and I have begun to be the friend I've always needed, to my own self. That's why it was easy to tell myself, when the comment about people running the other way came up, that it would be their loss.

What comes to mind is that my mother had people she controlled through money, me included. Everything with her came down to money that she had to play with. She was addicted to gambling; her need to control spilled into real life. I am so sorry now that I didn't have the energy to walk away from it sooner, but the reality of it is that I couldn't have. I was so used to seeking her affection in that way.

Through massage work, I got the feeling that I was contributing to people's well-being, something that my mother would only have allowed me to do for her if I'd agreed to the role of servant. I'd stopped being that when my father died. Getting back into massage at that point was important, but what I'm doing now by shifting away from it is important too.

I had come to depend on work for social interaction. Though for now I don't have a social structure other than through the out-patient clinic, that little bit is solid. Even when my time is up with them, the healthy pattern of checking in with a doctor once a month and a therapist once a week will continue. That was my mistake in 2012: I walked away from one doctor without establishing contact with another first. Being that I'm grounded now in a way that I wasn't then, it isn't likely for that to happen again. That is a secure thought too.

Some days the puzzle comes together more easily than others; 'checking the facts' is working particularly well today. Taking a little distance, I can see how people are made uncomfortable when confronted with mental illness. I was so uncomfortable with it myself that I convinced myself that I didn't have a mental illness, ignoring facts and behavior that were staring right at me. I am lucky to be here and in good health today. I am lucky that I've begun to 'trust in the process.'

I'm also lucky that I can trust in God now that I'm reaching a balanced state; I'm no longer just groping at the possibility of God's existence through mania. I needed to know that something greater than myself cared about me, when it seemed to me that my family didn't; I took leap after leap into mania to get that feeling of belonging. Now I feel accepted and loved as I am; what's more, it is becoming obvious that I was always accepted, by Nonna, for one. Just not by my parents. The grief work through the seminar brought that up.

Naturally I can't turn back time, but in the end there's no need to. I'm at the point of facing any attitude people might have toward me. For some, only time will bring with it proof that I'm worth knowing, that I'm not the person they fear, or have feared. That includes me. As time passes and I don't revert to past destructive behavior, I will gain more and more certainty that I can affect my own life in a positive way. I have to do the best I can through waves of anxiety and depression, to have faith in myself and in God, Nonna, and The Way, and make it through each day, one day at a time.

The more time passes, the less I'll feel the need to prove positive aspects of my character. But time has to pass. Addicts revert, often, and people in recovery have to expect the inevitable setback. There is no arrival point beyond which another setback might never happen again. But, with training, love, and patience, there are warnings which can be heeded, as setbacks loom near, and the worst can be avoided.

It would be great if I instantly found a job I like and can keep. Being that I wouldn't be doing it to gain outer approval anymore, it's likely that I would be able to keep it, and build on it. First part-time, then gradually more. It would be just as nice if not even nicer to find someone to be with, but there's no rush there either. Today, I am grateful for all I have, my home, my cats, my reliable car. The kid in me, who has hidden for so long, can come out of the shadows and play. She can grow into me, I can grow into her. It can start by making some ginger tea and preparing a light dinner.

Whatever happens next, a layer of bricks has been laid on top of a solid foundation today. Maybe there will be a movie to watch, maybe just more writing or going over notes, studying notes from class. I am not responsible for the fate of the world anymore, today. I count in my own life, and that is enough.

P~art~ S~ix~

With my cats' company tonight it's easier to write again. I've been nervous about it since getting hired to work at the Cranford library, a week ago. I don't start for another full week. The days have been long. I've been waiting to feel more grounded. Tonight might be the point at which I set aside my fear and begin to look forward to the future more. I have thought that I must always give something up if I am to get any of what I truly want. With enough respect for life in general, the amount of that which I must give up may lessen.

Tonight my neighbors are busy making noise. Furniture is getting moved around upstairs, a couple is having a conversation across the wall. I'll miss the thin walls least, when it's time to move on.

I didn't fight my way through life today. I moved with it. I ate fresh bread and butter. It was so good, I had two slices. It has been a long haul, this week. I have been so afraid of something going wrong when something has gone very right. A week ago I went on two interviews and was offered two jobs in one day. I took the library desk assistant job. It's ideal for me. Part-time and plenty of opportunity for socialization.

My knee still hurts. It's been six months. Leaving massage for good was the right choice. Writing with my left hand now, instead of my right, is a good way to slow down too. There is no reason to rush. The world is not coming to an end. My right hand would beg to differ, it would like me to do some furious writing so as to solve the next piece of the puzzle, and the next, and the next, guided by my mind and leaving the rest behind. Typing would be better yet, that part of me says. I might just solve the whole puzzle quickly, then, and get the reward that much sooner. But, like Alan Watts said, the point of dancing is not to get to a particular point on the dance floor, but to enjoy the dance. Same with the game of life.

My father wanted me to write with both hands when it became clear that I would have to write with my right hand in school. I said No. It wouldn't have been fair to have to do twice the work. Now it is an exercise: learning a new skill corresponds to starting life over. I am finally giving myself time, instead of wasting time by chasing after something I might need, which always turns out to provide limited satisfaction, and only for a short time. Writing longhand with my left hand, I get the chance to look at my thoughts as they come. Normally, once the thought comes, there is a mad dash to represent it as fast and as accurately as possible, as if time has already run out.

The cats are dozing. We played a little this morning. There is a good feeling in the apartment. The new leaf of the plant by the window is the largest yet, and looks very healthy. I am reminded of a book about plants which was part of the load our English tutor had us translate in the fall of '79. Plants are amazing. Cats too. They have their own mind. Just because plants don't have a brain it doesn't mean that they don't have consciousness.

This plant by the window knows it's safe to put out more and more leaves. Does this knowledge come from its roots? Does it come from the earth the roots rest in? Our brains draw oxygen from our lungs, and only then are able to fire off neurons which guide our actions. Plant roots draw oxygen from the soil, which needs water, but not too much or too little. Could the roots and the soil form something like a brain? In that case, plants have the potential to do something people can't do: expand their brain when the plant is moved to a larger pot. Our brain size is fixed, once fully grown.

It seems that my thoughts can be simpler, when I write with my left hand. I forget for awhile what a big disappointment I've been to so many people; I'm just allowed to play. I am comforted by my cats' presence. A broken part of myself is mended.

Another day at home with the cats. Just ate lunch, having some tea, practicing writing with my left hand again. As a child I conceded to writing with my right hand without making an issue of it. It just was what it was. Now it seems fitting to have a little fun with it. Pretty soon I will go back to typing, but for now it is a good thing to distract myself from serious thought by allowing part of myself a chance to unwind visibly.

It is very windy out today. Winds of change, very fitting. This time next week I will be behind the circulation desk at the library. I am so excited! In front of me in the glass bowl there are four oranges. I got them at the market in Kenilworth. I ate the other three already. They are not the best I ever had, but still good enough to mention. Now I'm having some tea. I have to wonder if other people's thinking would be simpler too, at first, writing with their non-dominant hand. Before they got good at it, I mean. To write as an adult and have it come out so childish is great, though I do have the urge to switch to my right hand right away, because with that hand I write more neatly. But today I have all the time in the world, so I am challenging myself to be patient. There is an innocence that comes with it. My young self is allowed a voice, more concretely. Here comes Vinny to talk me into watching a movie.

In a few hours I will be starting my new job. I've put one foot in front of the other, these past two weeks, waiting for it to start. It is a beautiful spring morning. The cats woke me up early, as usual. I am at ease. I ate breakfast, took a shower, got dressed, played with the cats, and now I am sitting at the table by the window watching Vinny drink water out of his favorite water glass.

I am getting fingerprinted this morning before I go in to work. That's part of starting over too. I had to do that, as did my sister, when we first came to Cranford. Yesterday I checked my email at the library and was happy to be able to put all the job leads into my Spam folder. There was a message midday from someone offering me massage work and it was a little strange to turn it down, but then I looked forward to today and it got better. My right knee is still not well enough for frequent exercise, never mind massage work.

I will need to ease into more swimming and walking again, though, as well as to cut down on animal fats in my diet. My bloodwork came back with high cholesterol. My doctor was worried enough to put me on a low dose of cholesterol medication for the next three months. I will finish the rest of the butter and yogurt I have, and not get shrimp anymore. It seems a shame to have to give up the yolk in eggs too, but I will have to do it.

I love knowing how at ease Vinny is, looking out the open window through the screen, now settling onto the back of his favorite armchair. There is nothing like seeing a cat that I love napping restfully, to the point of smiling, his ears still turning with the sound of birds chirping outside; once in a while a car passing through the parking lot will draw attention, then it's back to soaking in the sun with his back to the window. Kiddo is on the chest of drawers, laid out. I have scratches on my left hand, from days ago when I played a little rough with Vinny and he let me know it. I forgot that I'm not a cat too. The scratches will take a few more days to mend.

Less than two hours to go now till the fingerprinting. Both cats are dozing happily. I have made a point of slowing my pace down. Now I set up the computer only when I'm going to be typing in notes. For a few days I haven't even watched movies. I just wanted to become still and at ease before starting work.

Yesterday I caught up with TV watching in the waiting room of the out-patient center, and later in my regular doctor's office. I have no desire to hook up my rabbit ears. I save that for times of emergency, which thankfully hasn't been the case lately. Sitting by the window, I notice all the cat hairs on my black turtleneck. I will have to get them off before I go, with my lint roller, just in case I end up taking off my jacket. I took the time to have my slacks dry-cleaned last week. Now I notice it wouldn't hurt to use the lint roller on them too.

I made it through my first day at the library, and am getting ready to go back there again today. It's a good thing I didn't run out of sheets on the lint roller because I'm wearing a white shirt and I'm covered in The Kiddo's hair. It's another gorgeous day out. Getting fingerprinted was as fast and straightforward yesterday as I'd been told it would be. I had enough time afterward to go to the post office and mail a thank you letter and a couple of bills and get some more stamps.

I got an egg roll from the Chinese restaurant on the way back to the parking lot from the post office and went to eat it by Nonna's grave. I wanted to share my big day with her. They had removed the grave covers from wintertime and there were patches of dead grass where the covers had been. I didn't bring a candle this time but I did think of last November when I went there on the anniversary on my mother's death and did light a candle, and ate a couple of egg rolls. I'd also brought flowers and a pack of cigarettes. I took one out and lit it, and had three puffs: one for Nonna, one for my mother, and one for my father, although he'd given up coffee and cigarettes long before he died. It's still strange to think of my mother's dying right on my sister's birthday.

I have to get more ingredients for a new batch of cilantro pesto. It's time to do that heavy metal detox again. This morning I cooked up some of the quick oats I got in bulk at the store yesterday. They were delicious with a banana and raw honey.

I thought the transition from my yogurt routine would be harder. I'll have to eat the last one left in the fridge as a treat, maybe tonight. I already put the last stick of Irish butter in the freezer. I don't want to give up bread and I don't have to, since it doesn't influence my cholesterol level. I'll use raw honey on that. It's a good thing I already prefer turkey kielbasa to the regular one. White meat is better than red meat, my doctor said. I will miss shrimp the most. It was so tasty in butter and mustard sauce with a little brown rice or quinoa. Oh, well. Looks like it's time to fine-tune again. In three months I will get checked again and hopefully will be able to get off the cholesterol medication.

It really does feel like I'm starting over. It makes such a difference, to belong. One day at a time is key. There is no perfection, other than the enjoyment of each moment as it comes.

A very important part of the library job is being low-key. It will happen more and more. I told my therapist on Monday that something was in the process of changing in that the terror that used to be the norm is dissipating. I have been hesitant to mention my good fortune to anyone else these past two weeks, from a left-over anticipation of doom, which is what I've lived with for years. It had become my norm. It is important to set it down gently. Putting one foot in front of the other is alright, for the time being, in fact it is the only way to proceed.

Almost noon. The cats are napping peacefully, a freight train is passing, birds are chirping, cars are going by in front of the building. I won't need a jacket today.

I have been thinking about getting a proper desk but am waiting to see if it's just a passing fancy. The furniture I have right now works. The base of the old sewing machine, from Mr.Greulich's family, holds up the glass top that came with the coffee table that Mr.Greulich helped me put together. The base of the coffee table is sturdy enough to hold up Mr.Greulich's old moose head, which I've also inherited through the family. It's in the corner of the living room nearest the door, with a floor lamp which I keep turned on during the day, to set it off. I'd gotten the lamp for the plant which is now spread out along the window. It does best with natural light. It has been so sunny for the last couple of days that I really don't need to have the lamp on till the late afternoon, but I've gotten into the habit of it, so I'll go with it. As the days grow longer I may change that.

Today is the first day of another library book sale. I haven't decided yet if I should stop by downstairs after my shift. It will be packed right at that time. Maybe tomorrow. I am wearing the white shirt and cufflinks from the thrift store. It feels good to have a purpose. I think today I look like the grown schoolgirl that I feel I am. I have a tan vest over my shirt. I've put my bandaid over my damaged fingernail. I am taking care of all foreseeable details.

It's a beautiful day for a motorcycle ride. One of my neighbors just pulled into the parking lot on one. It woke Vinny up. He's drifting off again now. It's so easy to love him, and The Kiddo. Soon I have to get going, like yesterday, with no expectations, with patience and a delicious navel orange in my bag for a snack. Tomorrow I will get more at the farm.

I got a few things wrong yesterday at work, but in a way that will help me remember how to do things right the next time. I will ask for help again today. Soon I will iron my new pants. I took a shower and ate breakfast already. Another freight train is passing. Vinny is sniffing the fresh air, by the open window. The Kiddo has gone back into the bedroom.

The more I think about it, the more I'm proud of myself for applying for my new job at the library and getting it. There have been times when I've been a little embarrassed about my behavior there. I have been given a second chance. I am very grateful. The main thing, like my supervisor told me, is not to rush. Mistakes happen more easily when I rush. I felt a little like Tigger in Benjamin Hoff's books, so eager to impress. Today I will get another chance to practice being accurate rather than fast. I will need to resist the impulse to please through effort. *There are no uncontrollable impulses, just those impulses we choose not to control.* It's also important to take criticism well, a little bit at a time.

It's a gray Sunday. I return to my notepad. Being surrounded by books this past week, at the library, I had to notice how differently I've approached writing than is usually done. Now, more than ever, I will wait to promote it until I have a plan. More time has to pass before I can establish a credibility that I've never had. For now, it is important to continue to write and publish, but without rushing to promote any of it. Writing has been my lifeline. Gently, I need to shine less of a spotlight on it for awhile. With the many 'dimensions of wellness' to consider, not any one of them needs to carry the rest, as much. I did the right thing taking on part-time work, and in such a social setting. Lasting change takes time.

After an afternoon of daydreaming, it's still a gray day outside. My cats would like me to entertain them, though just our being in the same room together is enough. They look to me to lead the way. It's not dark yet, but I'm in my pajamas already after a hot bath. It has been a quiet weekend. I need to take the time to let the excitement of a new job settle. A shift so great for the better needs to be handled gingerly. Tomorrow I will check in with my therapist again.

Sometimes an unforeseen upset can lead to a stronger self, when it's handled well. Yesterday, in the early morning, Vinny fell off the bed. I think he was having a bad dream. It took him a few seconds to wake up from his twisting and turning, even on the floor. I coaxed him back onto the bed later, but at first he shied away. Not being able to comfort him right away made me very unsettled. It was pouring rain outside. I felt the old terror again, of impending disaster. I was planning to go into Elizabeth to the out-patient center to see my therapist and maybe sit in on a group. I was also planning to renew my prescriptions at the pharmacy across the street from the center. It took all I had to follow through. Luckily I got myself together and functioned.

Bear the discomfort and comfort will come, the Recovery *spotting* goes. Another one is *We are a capable and courageous lot, but we paralyze ourselves with fear*. My therapist confirmed for me that staying with the discomfort until it started to ease up was the right thing to do. Even in the grieving seminar there was a similar idea, of 'staying with the point of the pain,' experiencing one's grief fully before letting it go.

It came up for me later in the day yesterday that it's time to adjust my attitude in general when it comes to helplessness. I have insisted that I'm no better than anyone else. Now I recognize how important it is to see that I am no better than others, but better off than some, in any number of respects, and that it counts as a responsibility, once realized, to have more at my disposal. But my first responsibility must be to myself. I need to look to my own needs before I go take care of others.

Mental illness is not something to get over, any more than grief is, it is something to cope with. As I gather more tools to cope with my own mental illness, I need to stop comparing myself to others, to stop seeing what works for them and try to set up a similar setting for myself. I don't have the support of my family. Now with my parents dead I never will. That option is closed to me. I don't have a best friend or a confidant. That again, I have to live with. It's important to start looking for the things I can have, like my new job setting.

My therapist and I talked a little bit about shame, yesterday. We'll have to go into it more next week. I do cripple myself with overwhelming shame, even more so than fear. The anxiety that comes as a result of both can be debilitating. But if I bear with the discomfort something budges, like it did yesterday. I have to watch for what triggers shame, more so because people's comments that have nothing to do with me can trigger it. It is important at the same time not to disclose my being bipolar, at least not randomly, since there is no point in causing high shock value, but at the same time not to withhold it out of shame. In time I will find a balance when it comes to it.

This morning there's a noticeable change. I'm at the laundromat, drying my flannel sheets. The driers in my building, like all the washers except one, have been converted to use through a card only. I opt not to use my credit card to refill the laundry card, so I use the large-load washer which still takes quarters, and dry my shirts at home, but for drying my sheets I still have to go to the laundromat next door. The TV is on there, loud, but I do my best to ignore it, while I jot down what came up this morning.

I've noticed since yesterday that something has become clear: whatever I was worried about in terms of my new job was not based on reality, it was based on the mindset I was in, that of not being enough. Moving forward is about shifting out of that mindset. Every time I have made a mistake or disappointed anyone, the wave of insufficiency has come right away, and might still come again; it's so ingrained that it functions like a reflex, though it isn't one. In other words, it is something learned, this 'negative core belief' of failure, and it can be unlearned.

The word that came to mind this morning was "criminal." I have felt that I could never overcome the stigma of mental illness. For that reason, my life has been a series of compromises. I couldn't have a full life, I felt, due to my "record" of hospitalizations, so I've had to take scraps instead of holding out for what I really wanted. It's clear to me now that I felt punished, that I had come to accept that I was worthy of punishment. And I have assumed that someone would have to absolve me of my guilt before I could move forward, that it was my parents and only my parents who could do it. It was to them that I looked for forgiveness and absolution, neither of which they could give. With my mother's death, even the possibility of absolution seemed to have been forfeited.

This winter, when I was at the job skills course, I still felt that I needed to be approved of. I was better off in some respects than my classmates, but part of me still couldn't see me getting past the threshold of finding a job. Last week, my first week at my new job, I was terrified of making mistakes and thought I needed to prove myself. I thought I'd never make it. But on Tuesday my one coworker set my mind at rest, and since then it's gotten easier. Someone had done the same for her when she first started.

This morning I trimmed my hair and put on black slacks and my black turtleneck. My green socks will be visible only when I sit. I wanted to celebrate St.Patrick's Day, but in a low-key way. Last night, going to the community center to hear some Irish music was enough of a celebration.

Today I'm thinking about how my parents had to deal with stigma in their youths and throughout their marriage. They always had something to prove, to the point of instilling that in me too, after coming to the United States. Their way became my way, which they thought was natural. Maybe it was, but in a damaging way. There is so much to unlearn there. My modified, rebellious nature and my mental illness didn't fit in with their plans.

From my mother I learned that I would never measure up. I never saw that as her projection of her own insecurities onto me, in my teens and twenties. She was so adamant in her approach that I felt I needed to either bow to her, or to challenge her, both of which I did, in cycles. Disengaging from the *temperamental deadlock* didn't occur to me until I came across Recovery, which put across the idea that *in a temperamental deadlock, if one person lays down their arms the other has no one left to fight with.* Even then, by force of habit, I didn't leave the pattern altogether.

As long as my mother was alive, I never managed to disengage completely from my struggle with her. That made me feel like a failure, when she died. She'd told me that I had wronged her, that I'd been a bad daughter, that I would always be ill and that I would always need her. With her death, the possibility of absolution was denied. I was left with her charred remains on my conscience, until the slow but steady work of therapy started again, a year ago. Since then, much has changed. Today is a marker in that process.

The idea that I would always be a failure has been seriously challenged by events, in the past month. Today I don't feel I'm a failure. I feel I am someone in a functional recovery from a long illness. Manic depression is my genetic heritage, something to live with, to come to accept. The long illness I'm talking about is having to cope with my mother's abuse, over so many years, with the aim of letting it go.

I have something to look forward to now: the sense of belonging in my own life. I have lived like a criminal since my initial bipolar diagnosis, nearly twenty-seven years ago, but it's starting to look like it doesn't have to be the way I am anymore. I will make mistakes, I will continue to have limitations, but I will function, much like the majority of people around me do. Today there's the certainty that it's possible to unlearn what needs to be unlearned. The way to do it is to believe in myself and to listen to my own needs. Using a car service this winter was about that, when I had such high anxiety about finding parking in Elizabeth after the snow storm.

What I need to continually remember is that I need to forgive myself, and also forgive my mother every time the thought of her comes up. She entered a pattern of abuse early on, first by having to live with her father's being put in jail for political reasons when she was twelve, having to live with the stigma of being part of a blacklisted family; then in her life with my father, having to deal with domineering ways throughout their marriage, until he was diagnosed with Alzheimer's. She didn't have the inner strength to keep from turning the tables on my father then, and not to abuse him in turn. I have to accept that, to *drop the judgement* against her, to *excuse and not accuse*. It has taken me a long time to get this far. I need to follow through now, not only because it's the right thing to do, but also because it's the only healthy way to move forward.

When my mother poured out vengeance on my father or on me, when she needed to have me bow to her ways, it was because she couldn't help herself. I know that, today. The rut she functioned in had been set for too long. I was in it with her, and it's up to me to leave it behind as I rebuild my life. Body parts can be mended and patterns can be adjusted, at a rate I can handle. Changing the pattern of financial dependency is what is most challenging of all, but it can happen. My mother's need to dominate me in that way was something that she couldn't help. I have to step back and take *the total view* as often as possible, so that my own patterns can become healthy.

I have a choice, and realizing that much makes me responsible for my actions. I need to continue with the process of recovery, and have faith in it. It is the only way change of any lasting kind will take place. She needed to believe that being a depressive, as she was, was alright, while being a manic depressive, as I am, wasn't. She needed to prove that she was better than me. That is all past now, a pointless struggle that will fade away eventually. I must let it go at its own pace, and concentrate on my recovery.

The idea of functioning like a criminal came from being told that I was one, more or less, when I disagreed with my mother. She needed to feel superior to me. It worked, I did feel inferior, to the point of always trying to prove that I wasn't. It was a threshold I could not cross, until this winter, with the class, the job search, and now the job. I've been too good for some but not good enough for others. My new pattern is of actively letting go of that double standard.

Accepting my illness last year was the first step in breaking the cycle. Making the decision to stop doing massage was second, then going to the grief seminar, then the rest of the process this winter, all the while getting the therapy I needed. Much like building skills at my new job, the only way to do it was to do it, and I got through it because of my renewed faith in God, Nonna and The Way. Now, here I am, able to set myself back on track. There will be many more steps: getting healthier, building a social structure, correcting mistakes I have hesitated to face, like leasing a car I told myself I needed for my massage work, instead of buying a less expensive one. In good time, I will have the courage to address all my needs, one at a time.

I know more will come, because today I don't feel like a criminal anymore. For a person with a mental illness, or at least for me, being on a psychiatric ward is like doing jail time. It's a pattern that is reinforced every time it happens. I remember going to municipal court locally to help Tyler fight a towing ticket, and noticing how familiar most of the people there were with each other. They had roles to play, and they played them. In a larger scheme of things, who held what role was arbitrary, on either side of the law. The more important thing was how well defined everyone was in their own role, once set. Repeat offenders were common, attitudes of the law enforcers were foreseeable.

Everyone needs to tell their story to someone who will listen, even if the only outcome is being chastised for their actions. Breaking the law is one way to get attention, acting out against social mores is another. Customs are set partly to differentiate between those who will be accepted and those who won't. Subdivisions follow. What is difficult is crossing from one side to the other, once the roles are set.

Coming back to a setting that has been denied is hardest of all, and that's what I've been doing. It's hardest because it requires internal change. I keep saying that I've started my life over this spring, and it's true, because I am actively doing my best to reestablish credibility in a setting that has presented so many challenges to me. I've left Cranford over time in many different ways, but I've needed to come back to it because it is the one setting that may allow for full recovery. What I couldn't do out of shame while my parents were alive I may be able to do now: forgive myself and move forward, in the town I grew up in.

My parents, especially my father, had something to prove. Both of them had been part of the downtrodden. My being diagnosed with a mental illness derailed their hopes of a successful clean slate, and I became a disgrace. Financial success through my artistic talents or through marriage would have been my absolution. When neither happened, my role of a liability was set, in the family. Crossing back to a position of acceptable credibility has been a challenge that I just haven't been able to match or overcome, until now, this week, this morning.

Like the tide, the strength to see myself as worthy of a regular life comes and goes. Today, now, it feels like a more permanent shift has taken place. I am ready to move forward. I am forty-nine, a year younger than my father was when he defected to the West with my mother. I am getting a second chance, like he did. The major difference is that I am not severing myself from my old life, like he did, like I tried to do, many times over. I am moving forward at a rate that is inclusive. That is what will allow for lasting change.

Back at the apartment, the noise of the TV in the laundromat is replaced by the noise of a utility truck moving forward and back in the parking lot. Despite it, the sense of belonging in my own life is strong. I will be grateful when the noise stops, also for the sake of the cats, who are disturbed most by it. I make a point of not turning my own TV on loud so as not to disturb them. It is a courtesy that makes sense to me.

I find that people have come to accept noise at a rate I'm still not used to. That's another reason why working at the library is so pleasant. The quiet suits me well. I value silence that much. But it's important that I don't feel compelled to run from my home setting anymore. That compulsion used to be part of my pattern. Now I always know that it will pass. In this respect, I am luckier than my father was. Relocating is no longer necessary.

What I am reminded of this morning is the importance of trusting in the process of recovery. Today I am experiencing what in Recovery, the technique, would be called a *gain*: something more under my belt for when things swing the other way. The fear has been of being found out as bipolar. The circulation desk at the library is a public place, so there is that much more possibility of being "exposed".

Today, being bipolar is no longer a down side to my life, it just is what it is. That is a major change in itself. As I continue to *dare to make mistakes*, my work at the library will become second nature, in time. There is a lot to learn, and not everyone I work with will be able to teach me what I need to know. I have to be tolerant about that, even when I'm tempted to feel like a failure again for not being able to fulfill all my duties promptly. It will come, in time. For now, there will be more of the same: showing up on time, being pleasant, doing my best without stepping on anyone's toes.

On yet another peaceful day, the sense of belonging in my life has been extended. I will be going in to work soon, and I have plans for the weekend. I am mending what I can of my life, trusting that the tools will be there for me as I need them. This is quite a difference from the beginning of the week, when I was dealing with some of the residual terror of inadequacy that has been my norm for so long. Looking back over the past year, I notice that I have done my best to recover, and it's coming more easily. God, Nonna, and The Way have allowed for it. It's alright to be me.

As I get ready for another day of work, I feel ready to let go of more old patterns. Last night I had another visit from my mother in a dream. Today I am more ready to let go of her. Yesterday morning I felt like was on the run, like I have so many times before, as if I would be apprehended at any moment and have my lack of rights to a healthy life explained to me. Talking about it to my therapist helped, as did slowing down my pace when I got home. The apartment building was due to be inspected. I waited on the couch with Vinny. The inspector came and went. After he left I did some grocery shopping. I have been 'daring to exist', consistently; that's why so much anxiety has come up. Change comes with effort.

Today I am calm, aware of my old sorrow without the old fear of it. Acceptance of a life lived in the shadows comes as I stand more often in the light of day. My aim is no longer to find worth by seeing to the needs of others before my own. It has become, instead, to carefully dismantle the super-highway my 'negative core beliefs' have traveled along, all these years. There is nothing left to prove.

This morning I did my laundry, had a banana with my oatmeal for breakfast, and looked again at some pages in LIKE NEW. Details grounded me then, and are likely to continue to ground me now and in the future, so I took out my notebook again.

Vinny just slipped off the window sill onto layers of leaves and the lamp by the window. He is okay. Both he and The Kiddo went back to the scene of the accident, as it were, to search for clues. Now they've both gone into the bedroom. In time they will come back again.

In my bag I have two books and three movies I took out of the library last week. It's good to be reading again, starting with my old favorites, as ever. I was done with one of them just late enough on Sunday to miss the beginning of the grief support group. Being late isn't fair to everybody who got there on time, so I didn't go.

I will not be trying to appease my mother's ghost, however. Of that I am sure this morning, as I am of not trying to rescue anyone, anymore. My priorities have shifted, with my dismantling of my 'negative core beliefs'' pathways. I have reason to look forward to a healthier future, even if that means that certain needs of others who have populated my world in the past will be denied permanently. Changing my own patterns continues to be enough of a challenge. The needs of my mother and former acquaintances will fade with time.

It was alright not to see her one last time before she died, it is alright now to be civil but cool toward Tyler as I run into him in town. I am responsible for my own life and for the care of my cats, that's all. One of my responsibilities is to 'check the facts', regularly.

I have been so used to self-effacement that it is difficult for me even now to claim the right I have to put down roots in healthy soil and stay there, instead of allowing myself to be displaced yet again. The rent is going up again next month, I do not own my own home, but this home I have with the cats is fertile enough ground. I have stopped looking for yet another semblance of permanence. After I pay off my car, the budget will allow for two, maybe even three years of a simple, comfortable existence, with the work at the library. I will be a different person by then, less afraid. I can see that now, because it is already happening.

Looking at LIKE NEW again, I am sorry that it has taken so long for me to find a solid footing. I knew only to endure, up to my mother's death. But that in itself is a great feat. That is clear to me now. It was a twenty-five-year long-distance race. I endured and survived it. There were no others running alongside me, I just knew that I needed to keep going. Now I have myself to look after, kindly, with patience. There will be parts of the journey I will be able to share, some which I won't, but the race is over. I've rested, after my own fashion, for the past year and a half, now it is time to seek a new role in the world. I may always stay part-hermit, since it is in my nature to find strength in solitude, but it feels like I will be capable of taking part in a social environment now too.

The three plants that sprouted from the lemon seeds I planted months ago are doing well, enjoying the sunshine on the window sill, in the kitchen. Vinny is sniffing at the cool morning air coming through the window in the living room. I just ate my breakfast. The Kiddo is watching me from her vantage point on top of the chest of drawers. I accept my life for what it is this morning, in the way of a series of changes that link up to form the present moment.

Yesterday I had an enjoyable day at work again, with less nervous anticipation. The computer system is becoming more familiar to me, and the type of interaction I have with the patrons is ideal: respectful and considerate, with a certain distance. There is less to prove. Work is an excellent opportunity to practice detachment, which is a key lesson for me to learn.

I have been able to get a certain distance from my own life through writing. Attending to the needs of people I deal with directly while staying detached is a natural progression. A friend years ago said that we should all do well to be more like cats than like dogs, meaning to hold back a little. I am beginning to live with that approach.

Very slowly, I begin to see myself as able to provide a valuable service just by being polite and helpful. Living without glamor can only happen, for me, when I no longer need to be better than others. The competitive edge I was brought up with by my parents has been allowed to lose its sharpness; in time the stub of it, dulled to a harmless knob, will be all that is left of it. In the past I've tried to break it off altogether, resulting only in deep cuts to my flesh, leaving scars, and the fear of never being able to overcome the need to compete. Now, with more and more time passing since my mother's death, and with so much work through therapy since then, that edge that was so damaging in the past is diminishing as a matter of fact. The general attitude of harmlessness can take hold. A root system can develop now that was denied any real chance in the past.

I am able to distinguish between my chemical imbalance, which can be and is being treated with medication, and the stigma of mental illness. I am lucky that in my case there is medication which provides balance, without denying me the ability to function and work. It is the stigma which needs to be edged out slowly, being that it has become so entrenched. What helps me deal with stigma coming from outside is coming to terms with my own stigma.

I recognize now that part of my *temperamental deadlock* with my mother was my need to correct her. I needed very badly to have her acknowledge that she had a mental illness too: depression. She needed very badly to distinguish between her illness and mine, pointing out that she'd worked her whole life and had accumulated money. She would say that she was depressed "for real reasons." I needed to point out to her that she was wrong. What I see, now that time has passed, is that I engaged in our struggle with a certain amount of condescendence. No wonder she was irritated by it. I'd gone to art school and I had talents which people, including my father, recognized, so I was better than her in ways she couldn't match. She needed to judge me from her own level, and she did. As long as I was able to consider myself above worldly concerns, I was paradoxically stuck in my struggle with my mother. Doing massage therapy for a living was part of that too: I was becoming a healer, in my own mind; that would match my parents' work as doctors. There again, I was proving something, not just doing the work. When my mother died, that part of my life collapsed too, in increments.

Proving something to my mother, and before that to both my parents, was part of my arrogance. I learned arrogance from them, and excelled at it, as kids of immigrants often will. I was punishing them with my arrogance, but also with my neediness. I entered that pattern early on, just after Nonna's death when I was seventeen.

Arrogance was a way of life in my family. What I see now is that, for my parents, it had been the reason for being so motivated through the struggles and challenges life provided for them. They had found something noble in it: the pursuit of happiness in a way that would stick it to the government that had destroyed their families. Their intelligence became a weapon, second to their arrogant attitudes. I learned from them, a little too well. I was going to prove to them that I could do one better: I would live with the spiritual aspect of life that they had cast down, over time.

What I found out this past year is that living with spiritual inclinations isn't in any way about arrogance, intellectual or otherwise. People who contribute their time and effort to help others find their way, do so because they trust that they have a small part to play in a bigger picture, one that they may never fully see. But seeing the fruits of their labor isn't the point. Their wanting to help isn't arrogance. It is contributing in earnest to others' recovery from various types of damage done over time.

Until now, I have lived my life to accomplish something, and in doing so have stumbled and fallen, repeatedly. Until this past year, I have tried to match other people's standards. An attitude I've had over time is that if others help me, I must pass that help on. I only realize now that I've never taken the time to heal myself. To pull myself out of a deep depression a year ago I volunteered at a drop-in community center for people with mental illnesses, for a couple of months, until I'd built up enough anxiety to have to quit. I returned to doing massage, pushing my body so hard for three months between that, swimming, and walking most days, that my right knee, already lacking cartilage, nearly gave out. Then I spent the fall writing, needing to accomplish something again in that way too.

Then I went to the grief seminar. Only then did something begin to budge. I began to feel less unworthy. For Thanksgiving I went to be with friends who told me about the job skills course in Elizabeth. The same weekend I went to my thirtieth high school reunion and had a great time because people kept telling me I looked the same as in high school. Then I went to the job skills class and found out how strong my own stigma was, still. Afterward, through a great stroke of luck, I got the job at the library.

Here I am then, this morning, reconsidering my past arrogance. Stigma turns out to be related to it. Self-destructive 'negative core beliefs' are part of it too. I became very good at lashing out at myself, somewhere along the way. That's why it's been so hard to take compliments as they've come.

For the time being, life has become simpler: I've learned the basics of my new job, enough to allow for self-confidence without arrogance; I am cooking healthier food; I am playing with the cats more; my writing is shifting to a more constructive approach, and I am slowly able to return to physical exercise. Making note of all of it matters.

There enters a sense of danger when someone in a position of authority makes a mistake and I notice it. It happened the first week at work, a month ago, and again yesterday. That shows me that I have unrealistic expectations of any parent-like figure. That shows me that everything still goes back to thirty-six years ago, when it turned out, in coming to the U.S., that I didn't know either of my parents. They expected a lot of me but put it across to me in a way that made me nervous, rather than reassured that I could do it. And it was assumed that they were right, though what they said or did didn't always feel right. I was supposed to do as they asked, because I owed them a huge debt of gratitude for providing a new, better life.

A version of the same thing is happening now: I have been granted an opportunity at a new life, but when I see mistakes being made around me I panic, at first. I get the oppressive feeling that I will be held responsible for other people's faults; I'm not supposed to talk about it, either, or complain.

This is how I became intolerant of mistakes in the first place. If I wasn't allowed to make mistakes, why should others? In Recovery there are *spottings* such as *lower your standards and your performance will rise; we can't afford the luxury of temper,* and *we must dare to make a mistake.* Because I wasn't allowed to make mistakes as a young adult, it still feels unfair that others should be allowed to. That ties into *having temper at the illness.* Why do I count as bipolar when other people make mistakes all around me and are considered normal. This is an invalid question, I know, because *the illness is fate-appointed, not self-appointed.* It's important to make note of such residual feelings of unfairness, even as I become more and more able to function normally. Finding fault is an old pattern, which in the past was the first step to finding reasons to leave a job.

Yesterday it was a good time to *trigger-spot* again. *We are good observers but poor interpreters. We are a capable and courageous lot, but we paralyze ourselves with fear. Fear is the basis of the illness, a belief is a thought, and a thought can be changed, from an insecure thought to a more secure thought.* A secure thoughts now is that I will not be punished for making mistakes as a beginner, and that with a positive, inclusive, forgiving or tolerating attitude I will function that much better altogether. That is something I didn't know at thirteen, but now that I know it, having been able to step back from the situation, I can practice it. I can choose to be tolerant.

What was so troubling so many years ago was that I was supposed to make allowances for intolerant behavior coming at me, always to absorb more negativity, but not respond, not find a release. I was asked to be tolerant by intolerant people, in other words, by my own family. Patterns were set. Now, having stepped back from my life as it unfolds, once more, and having come to this insight, I get the opportunity to dismantle more of this insecure, intolerant thinking, first through writing about it, as I am now, then by living it out. *The method is simple but it's not easy.*

During my first week at my new job, I was attributing all of my anxiety to having to learn so much so quickly. Yesterday the sense of panic came when I thought I was being asked to solve a problem without being given the tools to do it. It was something minor, but I couldn't let it go. It tied in with my father's illness toward the end of his life, when I was trying so hard to help him lead as full a life as he could. He was forgetting so much. I didn't think of it as his making mistakes, because of his diagnosis, but the thing that was similar to yesterday's situation was that he still wanted to drive, for example, even when he'd started going through stop signs. That carried over into danger, and my mother and I had to do something about it. In the end we gave away his car and I ended up doing most of the driving.

I still have *an excessive sense of duty and responsibility* even in situations that are out of my control. I can learn more of what pertains to my job as I go. That has to be enough. What I need to let go of is the sense of unfairness, like being demoted from being a daughter for forcing my mother to stop driving when her vision deteriorated as much as it did. Every time I find fault with someone else's making a mistake, now, I have to step back right away and not compare myself with the person, or feel responsible for finding a solution to the problem. I don't have to "fix it", like I've felt that I needed to, so often. Every new day brings with it new variables, but I have to approach each day with the willingness to *excuse and not accuse,* myself and others. It is necessary to let go of the concerns of the previous day or week so as not to become overloaded. It becomes more important to concentrate on solving problems rather than finding the reason they happened in the first place. That's only important when it comes to machines.

It occurs to me that there's always room for more fine-tuning, which in itself implies the need for more tolerance. I need to stop running a race against myself. Thoughts have come and gone today, that will not come back at will. It doesn't worry me. Eventually the thread of one or another will pick up again. For now, after a light dinner, at home peacefully with the cats, I am grateful for my day at work. I have needed time in a social setting, but without my imposition onto others or theirs onto me. The timing is right, with nothing to prove, just being. I thought it might be therapeutic for me to be behind the desk at the library, and it has turned out that way. I feel that I belong, I am well, I am no longer in a rush, no longer denied. It's my doing, which I'm proud of. The shift is coming to a time when I will have more and more trust in God, Nonna and The Way. Coming this far has happened because of that trust, because of that faith. It is becoming easier to gather myself as I prepare for the next step, and the next. In time there may be a more permanent home, and a mate. I look forward to it.

With the cool air coming in through the curtain, with the bright sunshine, with the morning chores done, there is an easy feeling. Vinny comes into the living room to investigate, now moving toward the open window. The leaves he fell onto days ago are making their way back up to the level of the window sill.

Noticing the need for change is not enough. Most of what I've written has come through an act of observation, the establishment of much-needed distance from events in my life. Now I have the chance to go further. The silent terror of the past has subsided. It crops up daily, in small portions which I gently put aside until I can dispose of them on paper. Some of them slip away, promising to come back later. I still feel vulnerable, but it is arguable that only when we are exposed can change take place. I will go with that, and with the *spotting* that we must *act in a calm and cultured manner* at all times. Acting aggressively is something that I learned very well early on, but since it something learned it can still be unlearned, over time and with effort. That is my only aim. All of my basic needs are met, so I can concentrate on this. Letting go of more past strife is what needs to happen.

Years ago I talked to my therapist at the time about feeling polluted every time I left my parents' house. This morning on waking up I felt the way I used to feel then, but functioned. I had planned to go get some fresh bread for breakfast and some more cat food. I got myself dressed and went to the store. *It's not how you feel, it's how you function.* Now I'm doing my laundry at the laundromat next door.

The baker who sliced my bread at the store seemed as weary as I felt. It crossed my mind that any assumption I might make about what she felt at that moment was off, though, that I would be projecting my own thoughts onto her. Maybe she was tired but no more.

My parents used to criticize people based on their physical appearance every time we went out eating. I overstep sometimes from observing into interpreting. It seems this morning I will judge myself no matter what I do. I just have to ride it out. It's enough that I didn't stay in bed but did what I'd planned to do.

One thing that is probably average is my resentment. I come back to my first experience with disappointment, at the age of thirteen. I had expected so much of Americans, who didn't realize how lucky they were, it seemed to me. That attitude I had borrowed first from my uncle, then from my parents. This morning I'm struck by how much it's still there. As some older adults complain that youth is wasted on the young, I find myself resentful of others for their not being diagnosed with a mental illness, and I feel envious of people with supportive families. I am wasting time on negativity, in other words, while having trouble getting distance from it. I get upset when negativity comes across effectively in movies, as if some part of me were stained for life by it.

It's hard giving myself a break this morning, but I'm going along with faith in the process of recovery, going with the idea that *the resoluteness of the muscles will overcome the defeatism of the brain,* and another *spotting, it's better to be occupied rather than preoccupied.*

It's something like resenting having to get up for school in the morning, all through high school. It goes back that far. I don't know if I was as happy until my twelfth year as I think I was, or if I've just blocked out any negativity I might have had up to that point. What is for sure is that I've felt resentment since, for always being prompted to function in a way that would prove my worth, as if just being me was not enough. That's not just a bipolar thing.

However, I am struggling now to reenter the functional world at a sustainable level; the only way to do that is to *drop the judgement* in general. Fairness doesn't matter, my ego is of no importance, though it persists. I am still the pampered kid, though it's time to let go of that attitude for good. *Why me? Why not me?* fits. Every time I ask "why me" I need to substitute "why not me". It's hard this morning, but it does need to happen. Last year at this time I was staring at the ceiling all day, making it from hour to hour of extreme anxiety as my meds were being adjusted. I have to remember the *gains* I've made since then, and value them.

And then it hits me: I am resentful for having to be responsible for my own life. I thought I was done with that but it doesn't look that way. Being stuck in the old pattern is tied to getting ready to pay off my car. I have no duality about it, I know I will pay it off as soon as the bill comes, I know that it will be good for my credit score to have no more debt. But I still resent my mother for teaching me bad spending habits and then rubbing it in my face that I had debts. I have to let go of that. I have resentment in general about not having my own home yet. I feel angry with my mother for selling their home instead of passing it on to me, as might have been fair, and as my father had wanted. I find this morning that I still have a lot of resentment. But I do realize that if I want to, I can *drop the judgement.* I do have that choice.

It's not that the people I look up to and want to be more like don't carry resentment or biases. At different times, as I've gotten to know them better, biases and resentments have cropped up in them too. It's that being myself is good enough, so acting as if I'm not enough, out of a 'negative core belief,' is no longer appropriate. I don't need a whole new set of people to look up to, I only need to accept myself, and know that until I do I will be binding myself with the same locks that in the past used to be placed on me by others. I'm close to letting go but I'm not there yet. Trying to let go doesn't work either, because being in that mindset at all means that it's only the variables that change, not the process. Letting go in earnest is what counts.

Here I am now, back at home from the laundromat, having showered, after making the bed with clean sheets, having hung up my shirts and socks to dry in the bathroom, having dressed for work. I'm feeling a little better again, in the living room with my cats, thinking that I functioned well this morning. *Bear the discomfort and comfort will come.* This gives me hope that in time more resentment will fade.

There is medication and treatment for 'anger management,' both of which I'm partaking in, but clearly residual frustration will come up at intervals, and it's up to me to drop it. Medication, beyond a certain point, will only cover or mask anger much in the same way that painkillers mask pain. In time it must be addressed if healing is to take place.

So, how do I address my anger and my pain? By just showing up, for now. I can't actively make it go away; but I must also know not to indulge in it. I am training myself to live on a budget. I need to remember that it is working, directly because of medication and therapy. Up to my hospitalization last year I was still busy over-spending, like on books, and imposing my generosity on a friend in need. I can't deny it: it is medication and therapy that took away that urge. What I am doing by paying off my car is acknowledging that I bit off more than I could chew by going through several new cars in a few years. It was a game, it turns out, one that I can end now, not having overspent this year.

In time, I will be able to distance myself from that pattern. It is one part of growing up. In so many ways, I am as if a teenager straight out of high school. My car will be my first responsibility. In time I may earn more. But it is up to me. No one owes me anything, even if they've promised it in the past. I have enough to start out with. That is more than a lot of people can say. And having to allow time to pass between making a decision and being able to act on it is part of the process too, testing my resolve.

There is no danger in having to wait to fulfill a promise. *Feelings are not facts; they lie and deceive us and tell us of dangers that are not there.* The resolve has to be there to not "bite the hook" anymore, as in the past, that's all. It is that simple. Seeing the familiar prompt to act destructively, but not acting on it. Being angry helps nothing at all, besides being unattractive.

Without therapy I wouldn't have come this far, without treatment. I am dealing with anger and resentment that is as old as thirty-six years. I have to face it, then let it go; to no longer bury it, to find a way it can be used constructively, like ashes on a compost pile. I have to see my ability to use words that condemn turned over to the purpose of building healthier relationships. When faced with difficult interactions, I have to remember that *an insincere gesture of fellowship is better than an open gesture of hostility.* No ands, ifs, or buts about it. To find a way to be civil, without expecting a payoff.

I used to be afraid of showing anger or contempt. I buried both until my first manic outburst, twenty-seven years ago. In two weeks it will be that long since my first hospitalization, that I came out of with such a sense of shame. That shame led to more anger, more destructive behavior. I stayed in that patterns until my mother's death, a year-and-a-half ago. With help, I am making my way out of it, mostly by resisting old impulses, by letting myself be guided by logic rather than feeling. *There are no uncontrollable impulses, just those impulses we choose not to control.* Later I will go in to work feeling that I'm on trial, as it's been my tendency to feel, but logic and experience tell me that it isn't so, that each time I show up and function I am actively changing old patterns. Work is therapy, for me; the process has been consistent. I need to remember that every time I put down my weapons I am winning my freedom, including freeing that part of me which is still twelve-years-old and hasn't had a chance to grow up yet. *In a temperamental deadlock, if one person puts down their arms, the other has no one to fight with.* Armed to the teeth as I am now it can be a challenge, but there is the understanding that it's necessary. So I will do what's needed, with patience and a willingness to do with less.

I'm talking about something like humility, which I learned as a kid from my grandmother. Some of it has survived, and I must encourage it to develop again, if only to make her proud, when I can't see it as worthwhile otherwise. This is a turning point for me, acting with humility when arrogance is as old and ingrained as it is, in me. It's the only course that's worth it.

It is nearly noon, and I'll be heading in to work in less than an hour. Instead of turning back to bed, this morning, I functioned in ways that will allow me to *endorse* myself later, at will and as needed, with nothing to prove, even as I make mistakes. It has been a good morning.

Today I feel, as I have many times in the past, that I am living for the sake of anyone but myself, even if only my cats. They are a reason to be cheerful, to get through feelings of unworthiness, to make it through the day to the point of feeling I have worth again. It's as if I've been shown a healthy version of myself in the future, with a relationship and a full life, but I'm completely daunted by the prospect. This is something I work through every day: the overwhelming feeling that I don't deserve happiness. I function; I spend time showing my cats affection and returning theirs; I care for them cheerfully; I prepare for work and function well there, forgetting momentarily how unworthy I am, though in the back of my mind there's the thought that "if they knew" they would shun me as others have. It goes on like this, more some days than others.

It's as if my muscles atrophy overnight, and I need to learn how to use them all over again every day. That is my course for the time being. I do my best to be positive, although I know that the same weight is likely to be there again tomorrow, instead of saying Why me, why bother.

I have tried to face this feeling by treating it like a problem to be solved, but it isn't. I have also thought, in the past, that it's the medication talking, weighing me down. That may be partly so, but if it is it's entirely worth it – I no longer want to run away, to seek a lighter feeling by evading medication. My life is my own, it just doesn't look as lovely as others', in this self-deprecating mode.

I have conned myself in the past into thinking I'm not bipolar. Resistance to unpleasant truths has been part of my illness. No one is there to tell me to grow up, now. I show up in the world to get my cues as to how to do it, because I see the need for it. In this way I am like a hopeful recovering addict, my addiction having been to certain self-destructive behaviors and urges.

I have an extraordinary chance at a full recovery, though I feel unworthy of it. I may amount to something yet, just by being. I have needed proof that I am worthy, but it turns out that it's not needed. A hoax has been exposed. Its structure was all I knew. The illusion of defeat has been my life. I don't know how to go forward without struggling, other than just by showing up, day by day.

Last year at this time I was tempted to stop my medication because the side-effects were so strong, while we were working out the right dosages. I recognized the need to continue, thankfully, and stuck with the process until relief came, gradually. Now, work is part of my recovery. My inner critic is very resistant to it; it would have me collapse as soon as possible. It is telling me "Who are you kidding?" I need to continue forward anyway. *Symptoms rise and fall and run their course if we don't attach danger to them.* I have to remember that there is no danger in feeling uncomfortable. I have to remind myself also that intelligence is a gift, not to be squandered on destructive behaviors. Putting one foot in front of the other is all that needs to happen. In time, I will find my way to a productive life.

For now, everything I do to steer myself in that direction, even with effort, is worthwhile. I am not to be discarded for being imperfect. *Perfection is a hope, a dream, and an illusion.* As much as residual murkiness is likely to persist for the rest of my life, keeping my head straight, with faith in myself and in my own path, is worthwhile. Some days, making small inroads to feeling worthy is all that can happen. *Lower your expectations and your performance will rise* fits in here. "In former days", like they used to say in Recovery, I had more of my mother's negativity to look forward to during our phone conversations. Now there's just my 'inner critic.' I have to let go when it comes to this side of me, again and again and again. I have been addicted to negativity. It will take time to let it go more. I feel polluted because I am polluted.

But each time withdrawal comes now I know that it will no longer be replenished periodically, as it was in the past. Even with the discomfort of change, what withdrawal draws on now is the reserve of negativity within me, exhausting more of it all the time. In time, a balance will be struck at which this early-morning discomfort will be more bearable. My mistake in the past has been to try too hard to tip the balance in the positive direction through accomplishment, exhausting my resources quickly, then feeling unable to rise again to a functional level. Now I seek worth through moderation, by controlling the impulse to make broad strokes. It is already time for another platform of fine-tuning. I don't need to move on to another blank canvas, as it were. There may be no need at all to do that anymore. Making gradual, positive shifts is enough. I am worthy of the effort.

When I am at work I function well, and leave convinced that my worries in my time away from work are unfounded. Then, being so much on my own, I revert to introspection. It is not as scary as in the past, though. After all, I have been introspective all my life. It is alright for that to be positive again. Going step by step into my own life is what is happening, like a lucid dream. Given all that has happened in the past year, there is reason to be cautiously optimistic, which is more than I've been able to say in a long time. There is guidance. The thought of Nonna helps me consider my choices and find solutions to problems as I go. Every day, at least part of what I do is move through unchartered territory, which feels right. Trust and faith help me move through it.

www.ingramcontent.com/pod-product-compliance
Lightning Source LLC
Chambersburg PA
CBHW020908090426
42736CB00008B/532